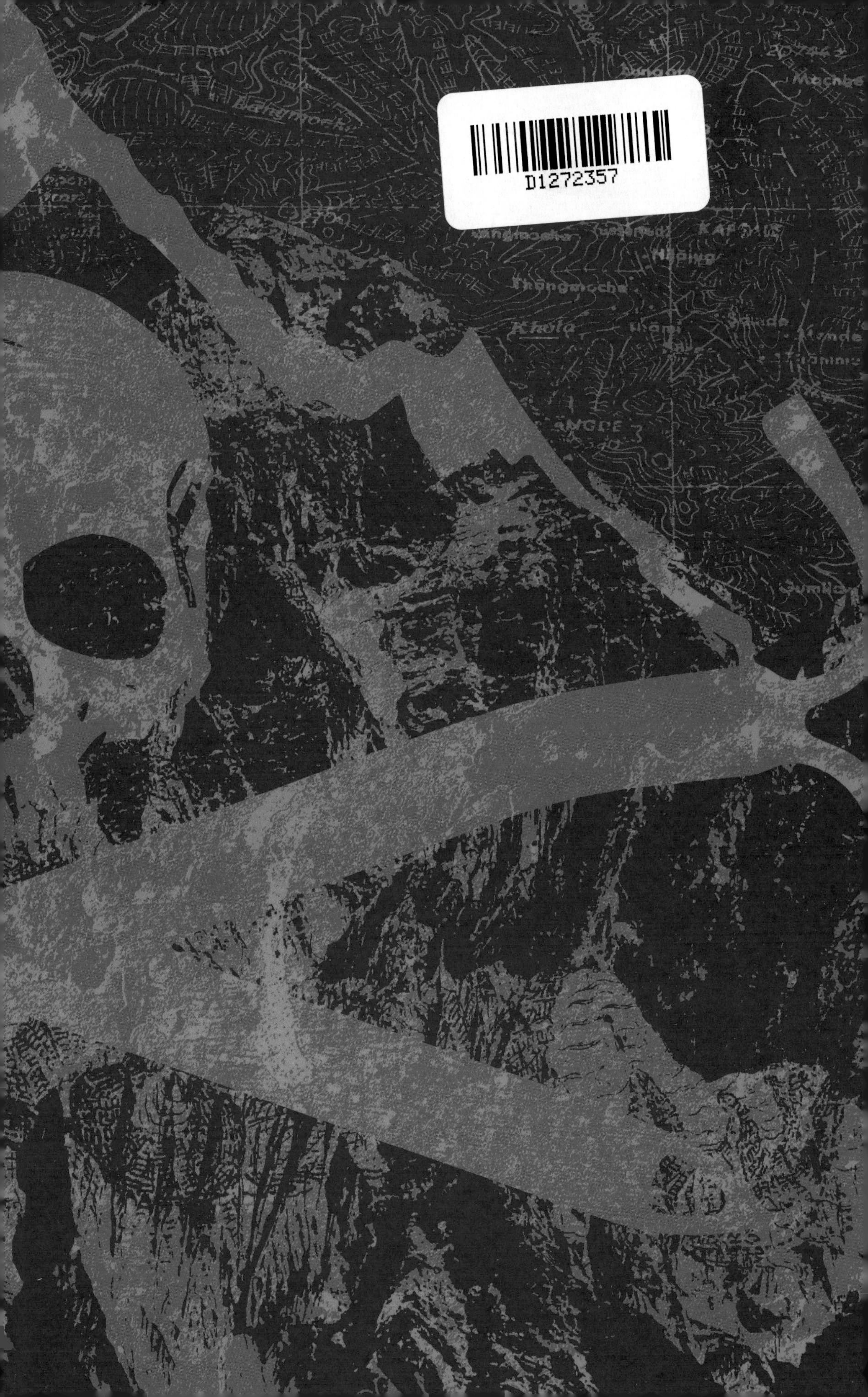

HIGH CRIMES™

"Not one element of this book is left to rest on its laurels. Sebela and Moustafa ensure everything has a deceptive shadow or drastic turn in it. You can't predict where this book will go."

—COMIC BOOK RESOURCES

"Every good story starts with a killer hook—or should that be ice pick?—and I'll be damned if this ain't the most original, creepy crime concept there is."

—ADAM CHRISTOPHER
AUTHOR OF *EMPIRE STATE* AND *THE AGE ATOMIC*

"The writing and art have a vertiginous quality as if at any moment the characters—and you with 'em—will drop down into a dark canyon abyss. Let me put it another way: if you're not reading *High Crimes*, we probably can't be friends."

—CHUCK WENDIG
AUTHOR OF *BLACKBIRDS* AND *UNDER THE EMPYREAN SKY*

"*High Crimes* is the perfect thriller—big stakes, damaged characters, dark pasts, and just the right ratio of humor-to-corpses."

—CHELSEA CAIN
NYT BEST-SELLING AUTHOR OF THE
ARCHIE SHERIDAN–GRETCHEN LOWELL SERIES

"Put shady individuals where the oxygen is thin and you get *High Crimes*, a thrilling, gritty high-altitude snow noir."

—SAM HUMPHRIES
(*LEGENDARY STAR-LORD*)

"*High Crimes* has a premise that made me jealous, characters I believe in, and art that ramps up the story. All I want is an adventure story with some depth, and *High Crimes* is all I want."

—PAUL TOBIN
(*BANDETTE*, *COLDER*)

"*High Crimes* is a wonderful comic about spies, scumbags, burnouts, addiction, and redemption at the end of the Earth. It's so good that Sebela and Moustafa can fuck right off."

—GERRY DUGGAN
(*DEADPOOL*, *NOVA*)

"*High Crimes* is a comic you can't afford to miss. Sebela and Moustafa have given us a truly inspired crime story that will be talked about for years to come."

—FRANK J. BARBIERE
(*FIVE GHOSTS*, *BLACK MARKET*)

"Real suspense, noir sensibilities, and a location so remote and dangerous it almost feels like an alien world. As rare as those elements are in modern comics, the main character, Zan, is something even rarer: a strong, flawed, obstinate woman who is heartbreakingly human. The storytelling here is so sharp that you won't watch things happen to her, you experience it with her."

—CORINNA BECHKO
(*STAR WARS: LEGACY*)

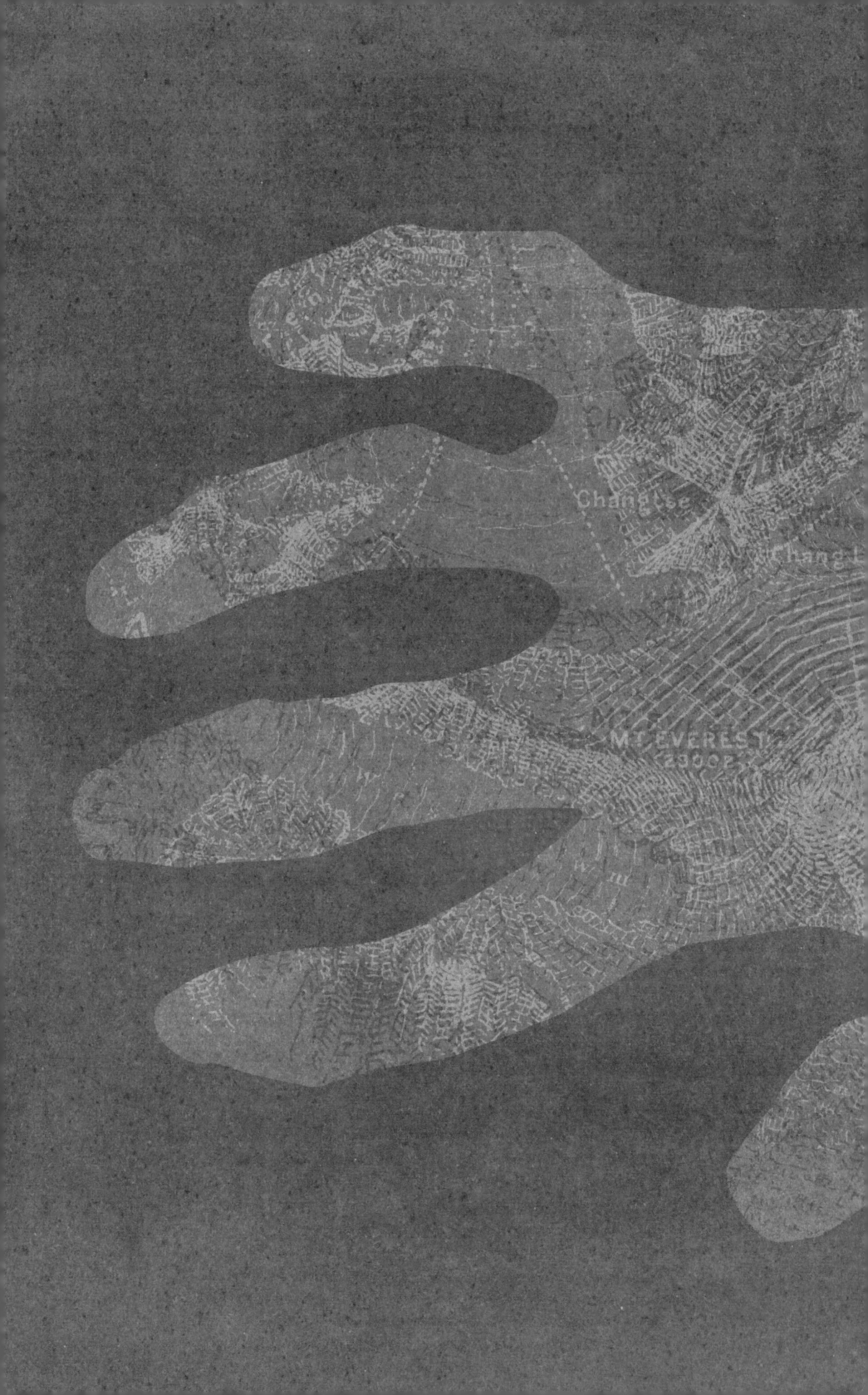
Changtse
MT EVEREST
29002

HIGH CRIMES™

BY

CHRISTOPHER SEBELA
and IBRAHIM MOUSTAFA

COVER ART BY

IBRAHIM MOUSTAFA

COLOR ASSISTANCE BY
LESLEY ATLANSKY
(CHAPTERS 7-12)

LETTERING ASSISTANCE BY
SHAWN ALDRIDGE
(CHAPTERS 9-12)

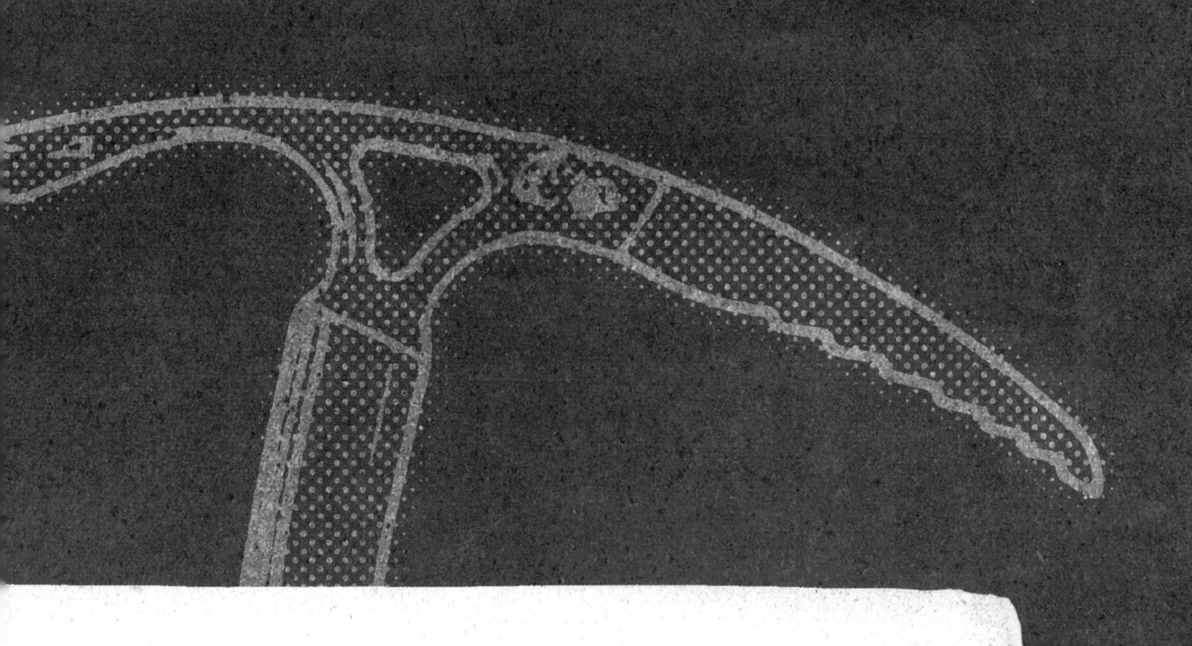

President and Publisher
MIKE RICHARDSON

Editor
JIM GIBBONS

Digital Production
ALLYSON HALLER

Collection Designer
NICK JAMES

Published by Dark Horse Books
A division of Dark Horse Comics, Inc.
10956 SE Main Street
Milwaukie, OR 97222

DarkHorse.com

First edition: July 2015
ISBN 978-1-61655-472-9

10 9 8 7 6 5 4 3 2 1
Printed in China

International Licensing: (503) 905-2377
Comic Shop Locator Service: (888) 266-4226

HIGH CRIMES

This volume collects High Crimes *#1–#12, originally published by Monkeybrain Comics, and "Strange Truths," originally published in Free Comic Book Day 2014's* Defend Comics *from the Comic Book Legal Defense Fund.*

SPECIAL THANKS

Thanks to Janna for her unconditional love and support through all of the late nights and weekends of work.

Allison Baker and Chris Roberson for believing in *High Crimes*, Jim Gibbons for bringing it to Dark Horse, and everyone who read the book digitally, shared it with friends, retweeted links, bought T-shirts, and said hello at conventions. You're all wonderful.

Bob Schreck for putting me on the right path.

Joe Keatinge for introducing Chris and me.

And Chris, for conceiving this crazy, amazing idea, and being a great friend throughout the process of bringing it to life.

—Ibrahim

Chris and Allison, who Sherpa'ed this book from a burning idea into an actual comic when no one else would.

Matt and Kel, who saved my life and made my own impossible dream possible.

Joe Keatinge, who introduced me to Ibrahim one hot summer day and changed both our fates.

Terry Tyson, who was the first one to get excited about the idea and whose willingness to share his climbing knowledge made this book what it is.

Laurenn McCubbin, who kicked my ass and told me to get back in there.

Alex Getchell, who accidentally named the Strange Agents.

Brian Churilla, for mental support and severed hands. Sorry I barfed in your yard.

Zan McQuade, whose name I stole and who graciously let me steal it.

Mom, who always supported the climb even when it looked like I was walking off a cliff.

Ibrahim, the greatest climbing partner a guy could ever ask for.

—Christopher

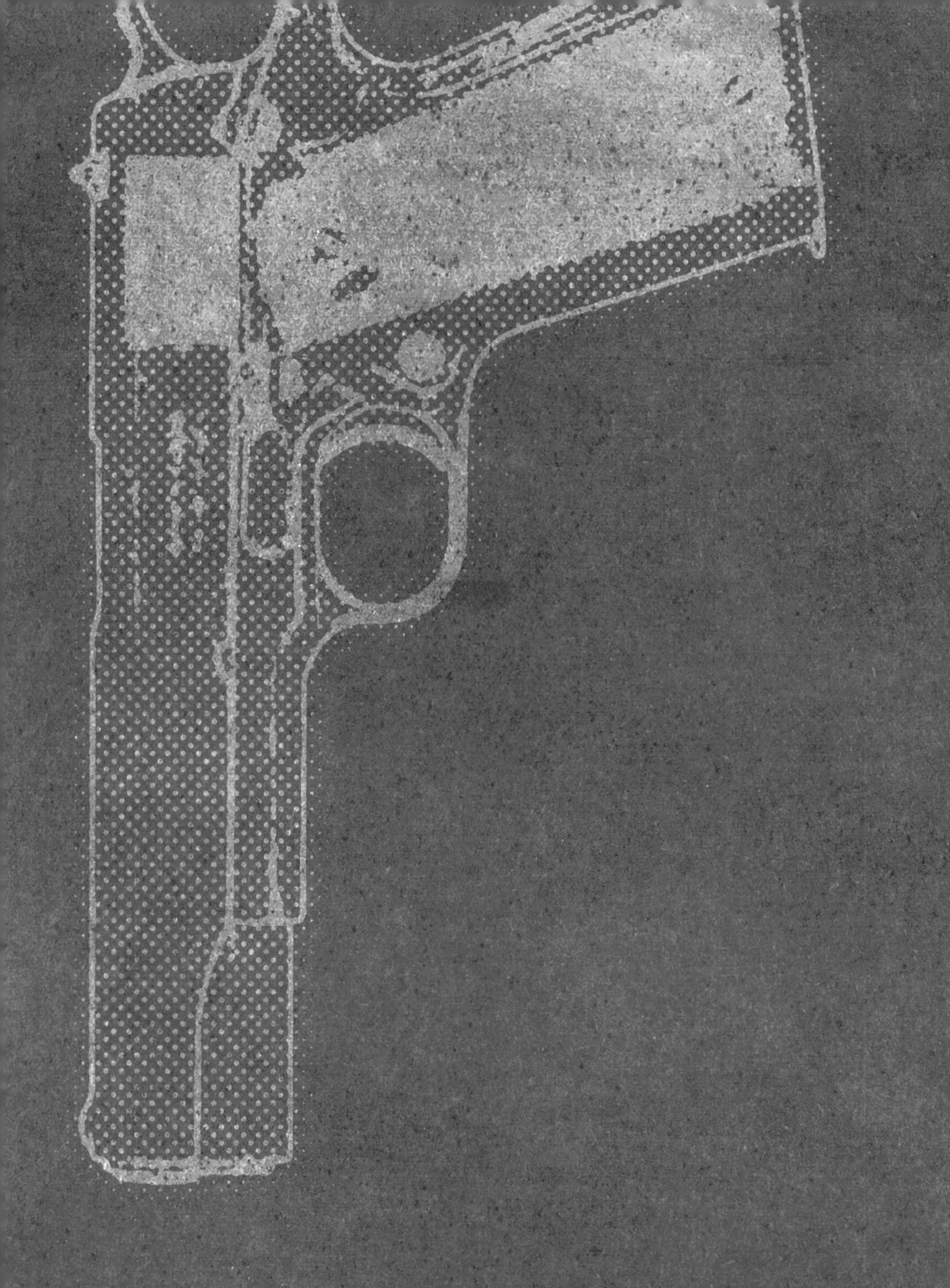

ADDITIONAL SECURITY INFORMATION

ound documents—Classified books or pamphlets, the pages of which are permanently and securely bound together so that e pages thereof cannot be removed without damage or mutilation, shall be marked with the classification assigned to the ocument at the top and bottom on the outside of the front cover and back cover, title, first and last pages and all printed, or written pages which contain classified information, including the reverse side, if used.

orrespondence and unbound documents—Correspondence and other documentary material not permanently and securely ound together shall be marked with the appropriate classification at the top and bottom of each page which contains assified information, including the cover page, if used. The marking shall be placed so that it will not be hidden from ew when the pages are clipped or stapled together.

etters of Transmittal—A letter transmitting defense information shall be marked with a classification at least as high as ... when appropriate, shall indicate that upon removal of classified ...

TOP SECRET / EYES ONLY

I have a problem with Chris Sebela and Ibrahim Moustafa.

To be clear—and if I'm about to start a lifelong feud or something with the two of them, then I think it's best for all involved that I *am* clear; I'm sure you agree—my problem is not with their work. Nor is it a problem with their art, and *High Crimes* is very much a work of art.

It's not a problem with Sebela or Moustafa personally, either. The handful of times I've met Ibrahim, he has been nothing less than absolutely charming. Even Chris, who has gone to near-Herculean efforts to cultivate an air of genial misanthropy (the man has weaponized his beard, for God's sake), is, in point of fact, one of the most thoughtful and smart guys it's been my pleasure to get to know in recent years.

They're lovely people, that's what I'm saying. So it's not that.

And it's not a misguided jealousy on my part about their attention to detail and their obvious love of research, both so abundant throughout this story. Coming from a research junkie like myself, that's begrudging, I'll admit it, but it's true, and it is worthy of both respect and admiration. Case in point: Chris is the only person with whom I've ever actually been able to have a Krakauer vs. Boukreev argument about the tragic events on Everest during the 1996 season. That's the kind of argument you can only have with someone who's a fellow armchair climber, with someone who's done the deep dive into research, history, and lore.

But it's not any of that, either.

What it is, is the problem that comes from knowing that there are two other men in love with the same person you are. We're all in love with the Mountain. We're all in love with the Goddess. We're all in love with Everest.

And I'm honestly kinda jealous that they got to go out with her first, and that they've shown her such a good time, and that maybe now I'm never going to get my chance to ask her out myself, let alone take her to dinner and a movie.

(Before we cry sexism, I would point out that Everest is commonly feminized. The Sherpas refer to the Mountain as Chomolungma, "The Mother of the World." And yes, pages upon pages could be written about the Western need to "conquer" her. That feminization is also something worth noting when you consider that Moustafa and Sebela's protagonist is a woman, a very deliberate and considered choice on their parts.)

So, yes, I wanted to ask her out, and I got cold feet, and other things came up, and I chickened out, and Chris and Ibrahim got there first. And that would be okay, too, honestly, but dammit, then they had to go and tell a brilliant damn story.

I'm having a hard time with that, I have to admit.

You're going to have a similar problem. Falling in love with Zan is, perhaps, optional, but few of us get away without being seduced by the Mountain.

Enjoy the climb.

Greg Rucka
Portland, Oregon
March 2015

LEAVE THIS SPACE BLANK

TYPE OR PRINT

LAST NAME

FIRST NAME

MIDDLE NAME

SEX

HT.

SIGNATURE OF PERSON FINGERPRINTED

CONTRIBUTOR AND ADDRESS

ALIASES

HAIR

DATE

SCARS AND MARKS

AMPUTATION

YOUR NUMBER

PLACE

LEAVE THIS SPACE BLANK

SIGNATURE OF OFFICIAL TAKING FINGERPRINTS

DATE

PLACE FBI NUMBER HERE

CLASS.

REF.

CHECK IF NO REPLY IS DESIRED

1. RIGHT THUMB

2. RIGHT INDEX

3. RIGHT MIDDLE

4. RIGHT RING

5. RIGHT LITTLE

6. LEFT THUMB

7. LEFT INDEX

8. LEFT MIDDLE

9. LEFT RING

10. LEFT LITTLE

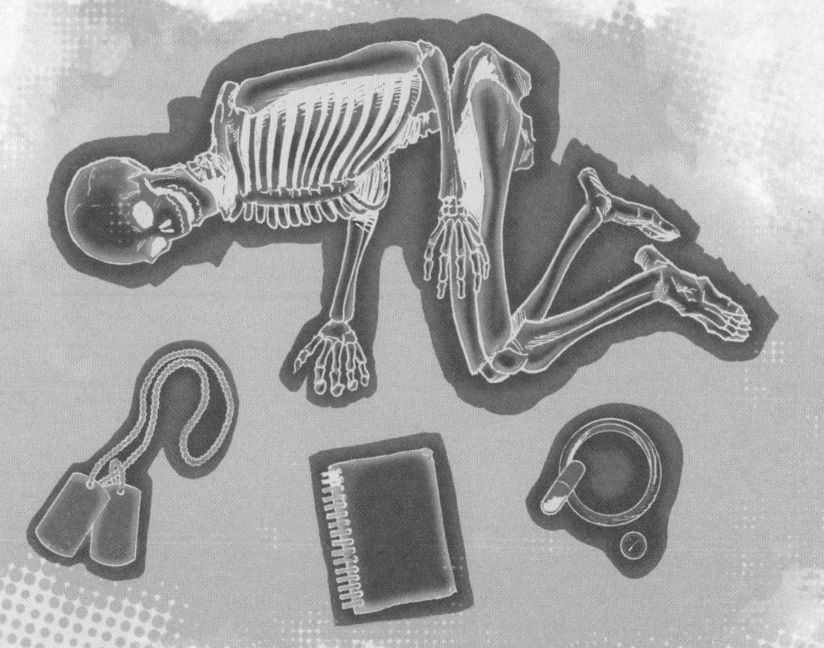

MOUNT EVEREST.
SOUTHEAST RIDGE.

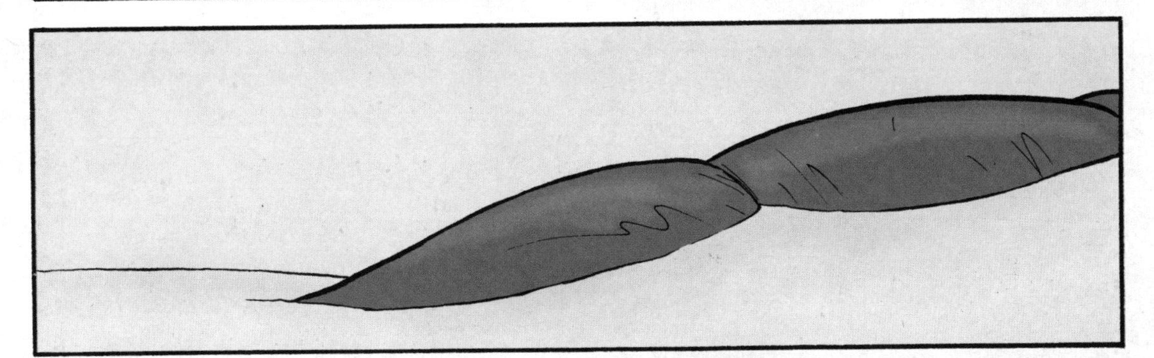

PRICE!

PRICE!

HEY, PRICE!

PRICE! THE HELL'RE YOU DOING OVER THERE? WE'RE ABOUT TO HEAD UP TOP.
AND MR. CREELEY'S GONNA NEED A BIT MORE HELP.
SURE THING.
SORRY, JIM. THOUGHT I SAW SOMETHING. I'M GOOD TO GO.

BESIDES, I DON'T TRUST THESE CLOUDS TO HOLD OUT FOR TOO MUCH LONGER.
GREEN LIGHT, FOLKS!
LET'S GET MOVING. YOU'VE GOT ABOUT TWENTY MINUTES TO SPEND UP THERE, TOPS.
TAKE YOUR PHOTOS, WAVE YOUR FLAGS, THEN GET READY TO START HEADING DOWN.

WE'RE 'BOUT TWO HOURS BEHIND AND WEATHER'S MOVING IN. I DON'T WANT ANY ARGUING FOR MORE TIME.

"YOU SHOULD BE PROUD. YOU DID IT. BUT THERE'S STILL A LOTTA WORK AHEAD OF US.
"YOU PAID US TO GET YOU UP HERE. MORE IMPORTANTLY, TO GET YOU BACK HOME INTACT...
"...AND THE ONLY THING HARDER THAN GOING UP IS COMING BACK DOWN ALIVE."

ONCE UPON A TIME,
I FUCKED IT ALL UP.

GODDAMMIT.
THE NIGHTMARE VISITS ABOUT ONCE A WEEK.
A FEW YEARS AGO, IT WAS EVERY NIGHT.
I HEAR THE GASPS, THE BOOS. I CAN PICK OUT EACH DISAPPOINTED SIGH.
I BLEED INTO THE SNOW.
THE MIND IS FUNNY. I CAN REMEMBER EVERY DETAIL OF THAT MOMENT.
IT'S EVERYTHING ELSE THAT'S FUZZY THESE DAYS.

IT'S KIND OF ANNOYING. SO MANY PERFECT DAYS I'D BE HAPPY TO RELIVE.
JUST GHOSTS OF THEM LEFT. CRASHED AND BURNED, LIKE ME.

FOR A LONG TIME, THIS NIGHTMARE HAUNTED ME.

BUT THESE DAYS IT ALMOST FEELS LIKE A BEAUTIFUL DREAM.

ONCE UPON A TIME, I HAD IT ALL, WITH GOODWILL TO BURN.
SO I BURNED THROUGH THAT TOO AND IT TURNS OUT THERE *WAS* A BOTTOM ALL ALONG.
BY THEN I WAS MOVING TOO FAST TO REALIZE I'D ALREADY SMASHED STRAIGHT THROUGH IT.
The ENGLISH AIR
122
1838
EVEREST

OI! SNOW BUNNY!
COME ON OVER. WARM YOURSELF ON MY LAP.

YOU'RE GROSS, SOPHIE.
PISH-POSH, YOU KNOW YOU LOVE ME, ZAN. *COME*, SIT. I'VE MISSED YOU SO.

BARKEEP!
SO, WHAT WAS IT THIS TIME? HOLDING SOME RICH TOURIST'S HAND UP K2?
NANGA PARBAT.
AND WE JUST PROVIDE SUPPORT AND SUPPLIES.
IF THEY CAN'T CLIMB, WE'RE *FREE* TO KICK 'EM BACK HOME.

THAT'S A *LOT* OF WORDS JUST TO SAY YES.
WHAT'LL IT BE TODAY, LADIES?
HELLO AGAIN, DANIEL. I WILL BE HAVING ANOTHER ONE OF *THESE* MIRACLES. BRING ZAN HER USUAL ROTGUT. REPEAT UNTIL WE SAY STOP.
HEY...

STILL SHAGGING THE HELP, I SEE?
SHUT *UP*. CAN I PLEASE HAVE *ONE* SECRET YOU DON'T KNOW ABOUT?
IN THE HISTORY OF YOUR SECRETS I'VE KEPT, THIS ONE'S *PRETTY* MINOR.

NOW SPILL YOUR GUTS. WE'VE GOT DRUNK TO GET.
I *HATE* YOU, SOPHIE. I TRULY DO.

TRIBHUVAN AIRP
BEEEEP
"HELLO? A HASKELL PRICE CALLED? ABOUT MY BROTHER? SEAN LAFOUR? YOU FOUND HIS BODY?"
BEEEEP
"LISTEN, MATE. DON'T CALL US ANYMORE. WE'VE ALREADY CONTACTED INTERPOL. THEY'RE LOOKING INTO YOU, SCUMBAG."
TAXI
BEEEEP
"$10,000 IS QUITE A LARGE SUM OF MONEY, YOU UNDERSTAND. AFTER ALL, IT'S JUST A BODY. IT'S NOT AS THOUGH YOU HAVE TO BRING HIM DOWN ALIVE."
ENTRANCE
BEEEEP
"WE'VE RECEIVED THE FINGERPRINTS AND YOUR PHOTOS OF THE LOCKET. OUR ATTORNEY WILL BE IN CONTACT TO WORK OUT THE DETAILS."
INDIA
BEEEEP
"GRAVE ROBBERS. THAT'S ALL YOU ARE."
BEEEEP
CL-CLICK
BEEEEP
"GO ON AND LEAVE HIM UP THERE. LET HIM ROT FOR ALL I CARE."
BEEEEP
"MY WIFE'S BEEN DEAD FOR FOUR YEARS AND NOW YOU WANT ME TO PAY YOU FOR HER...HER CORPSE?"
"WHAT KIND OF SICK JOKE IS THIS?"

YOU *ARE!* YOU'RE TOTALLY IN LOVE.
OH, FUCK OFF. I'M IN *LIKE.* I HAVEN'T BEEN IN LIKE IN FOREVER.
PERILS OF MY FUGITIVE LIFESTYLE.

I'VE SPENT THE LAST THREE YEARS RUNNING FROM HOME, FROM THE PRESS, FROM EVERYTHING.
WHY SHOULDN'T I RUN *TOWARDS* SOMETHING?
EVEN IF IT *IS* DANIEL.
DUDE, CHECK IT OUT.
JESUS. YOU'RE SO *DEEP* WHEN YOU GET PISSED.

AW, FUCK. HERE WE GO AGAIN.
WHAT? HERE WHAT GOES?
THAT DOUCHE IN THE BEANIE. I THINK HE RECOGNIZES ME.

"WHAT'S THAT MAKE, ZAN? THE THIRD ONE THIS YEAR?"
"FOURTH. I'M *NEVER* GOING TO GET AWAY FROM THIS SHIT.
"I'M TRAPPED. STUCK AS ME."

CALM DOWN. I'VE GOT THIS ONE.
NOT DRUNK ENOUGH. NOT NEARLY DRUNK ENOUGH.

WHAT DO *YOU* IMAGINE YOU'RE ABOUT TO DO?
BECAUSE WHATEVER IT IS YOU *PICTURED* HAPPENING? THIS IS AS CLOSE AS YOU'RE GOING TO GET.
WHOA, WHAT DID I--
GO ON, YOU FILTHY COLONIST.

SUZANNE, GET YOUR BUTT UP.
WE NEED TO CHAT.

The ENGLISH AIR
GIRL, YOU ARE A WALKING CATASTROPHE LATELY. FRANKLY, I AM AMAZED YOU CAN CLIMB OUT OF BED EVERY MORNING WITHOUT BREAKING YOUR NECK.
GOOD TO SEE YOU TOO, HASKELL.
LET'S GO. I YELL BETTER WHEN I'M WALKING.

HOTEL
--AND I COME BACK TO THE OFFICE AND THE FREEZER PADLOCK IS SITTING ON THE DAMN DESK.
MAYBE IF YOU LEARNED THE LANGUAGE YOU COULD HAVE WRITTEN A HELPFUL NOTE TO ANY THIEVES.
I FORGOT. I SO HOPE YOU CAN FIND IT IN YOUR HEART TO FORGIVE ME.

IT'S NOT JUST THAT. IT'S EVERYTHING. STILL GETTING HIGH, STILL GETTING DRUNK, LIVING DAY TO DAY. WHAT ARE YOU DOING WITH YOURSELF?
WHAT? I'M DOING THE SAME THING I WAS WHEN WE MET.
EXACTLY.

I DON'T CRITICIZE HOW YOU LIVE, HASKELL. YOU'RE MY PARTNER, NOT MY DAD.
RIGHT--

--SO WHEN I TELL YOU TO STRAIGHTEN UP OR PACK YOUR TRASH? YOU SHOULD KNOW I ACTUALLY MEAN IT.
UH-HUH. EVEN IF WHAT WE'RE DOING ISN'T TECHNICALLY ILLEGAL, WE'RE STILL DIRTY AS HELL. WE GO DOWN TOGETHER.
CAN WE GET TO WORK?

"SO... HOW WAS IT?"

EVEREST? THE SAME. THERE'S JUST MORE PEOPLE AND MORE TRASH PILING UP.
YOU OUGHT TO GO. BEFORE IT GETS COMPLETELY RUINED.
SEASON'S ALMOST OVER. MAYBE NEXT YEAR.

YOU KEEP MYTHOLOGIZING THAT MOUNTAIN AND YOU'RE GOING TO END UP DISAPPOINTED. YOU'RE MORE THAN READY FOR IT. IF IT--
"WHY, IF IT WAS AT SEA LEVEL, MY GRANDKIDS COULD RUN UP IT." I KNOW.

SUZANNE, ONCE YOU SUMMIT, YOUR RATES GO UP. YOU CAN START GUIDING FOR A REPUTABLE OUTFIT, MAKE YOU SOME REAL MONEY.
IT'S YOUR BRASS RING.
WRONG, HASKELL.
EVEREST 24,000FT.

EVEREST IS MY GOLDEN TICKET.
TAKES ME THE HELL OUT OF THIS LIFE.

SO YOU CLIMB UP A MESS AND COME DOWN A PERFECT GIRL? SOMETHING LIKE THAT?
I COME DOWN AND KEEP ON GOING. LEAVE ALL THIS BEHIND. NO MORE DRUGS, NO MORE "ADVENTURE CONSULTANTS," NO MORE SHAKING DOWN STRANGERS TO SEND THEIR LOVED ONES' REMAINS BACK HOME.
NO MORE ZAN JENSEN.
POLICE
RIGHT.
YOU PICK YOUR NEW NAME YET?
I'VE ALWAYS LIKED EMILY.
THERE HE IS. HANG BACK.

EVENING, TENZING.
AHA, MR. PRICE. PERFECT TIMING. MY DINNER HOUR IS NEARLY OVER.
WHAT DO YOU HAVE FOR ME?
SEVEN SETS OF PRINTS, ALL IN SEARCH OF A NAME.
ALONG WITH YOUR FEE, OF COURSE.
MY, MY. YOU CERTAINLY HAVE BEEN BUSY THIS SEASON.
IT'S A GROWTH INDUSTRY.
MORE CLIMBERS, MORE AMATEURS, MORE BODIES LEFT UNCLAIMED ON ALL THOSE PEAKS.
MORE MONEY FOR US ALL.
MAY I SAY, YOU'RE GETTING QUITE SKILLED AT FINGERPRINTING, MR. PRICE.
THOUGH I IMAGINE IT'S EASIER WHEN THERE'S NO ONE ATTACHED TO THEM.
EVEREST 24,000 FT.
SUMMIT
MAKALU
EVEREST 22,600
"I'LL SCAN THEM IN AND SEND MY ASSISTANT OVER WITH THE I.D. RESULTS IN THE MORNING."
"USE A COURIER, TENZING. WE DON'T NEED ANYONE ELSE KNOWING ABOUT THESE."
"OF COURSE, MR. PRICE. NO NEED TO WORRY...
Renner, George
Ht. 6'2"
Wt. 195lbs
Hr. Clr. Br.
Eye Clr. Bl.
Mars, Sullivan

"...I'M THE ONLY ONE WHO WILL SEE THESE."
BLAM!
SULLIVAN FUCKING MARS.
WE'VE GOT YOU NOW, COCKSUCKER.
I TOLD YOU YOU COULDN'T HIDE FOREVER.
Locating....
Locating....
Mars, Sullivan
Located: Kathmandu, Nepal

ON YOUR FEET!
BLAM! BLAM! BLAM!
PLEASE DON'T BE DEAD, SULLY.
I STILL WANT TO PULL YOUR SECRETS OUT, ONE TOOTH AT A TIME.

WELCOME TO FIRST STRIKE.
THIS IS AN ALL-WEATHER SCENARIO. GEAR'S WAITING IN THE ARMORY.
YOU'VE GOT FIFTEEN MINUTES TO REGROUP IN THE BARN.
YOU'RE HEADED TO NEPAL.

SIR? THERE'S NOTHING IN OUR ORDERS ABOUT NEPAL.

BLAM!
NEW ORDERS.
FOURTEEN MINUTES.

"SEVEN'S A LUCKIER NUMBER ANYHOW."
AGENTS, LET ME INTRODUCE YOU TO YOUR TARGET: SULLIVAN MARS.
YOU HAVE THE NEXT TWELVE HOURS TO BURN THIS MAN'S *LIFE* INTO YOUR BRAINS.

TWENTY YEARS AGO, MARS WAS ***THE*** PERFECT PRODUCT OF THIS MAN'S AGENCY. EMPIRES TOPPLED, GOVERNMENTS OVERTHROWN, A WETWORK LIST LONGER THAN YOU ARE ***TALL.*** LEGEND TIME.
THEY ENTRUSTED HIM WITH THE DIRTY LAUNDRY OF THE FREE WORLD AND HE RAN. DISAPPEARED OFF THE GRID.
UNTIL THIRTY MINUTES AGO. SOME UNLUCKY ASSHOLE IN THE KATHMANDU POLICE DEPARTMENT JUST RAN HIS PRINTS. NOW WE PLAY FETCH.

"IF HE IS DEAD, FIND THE BODY. BRING IT HOME. DON'T LEAVE ANY VALUABLE PIECES BEHIND.
"THIS OPERATION IS OFF THE BOOKS. WE DON'T EXIST. DON'T DRAW A SCENE, BUT, BY ALL MEANS, HAVE ***FUN*** WITH IT.
"SCRUB THE SCENE. CIVILIANS, POLICE, ANYONE WHO EVEN KNOWS HIS NAME IS ALREADY A LIABILITY.

"REMEMBER, MARS WENT ROGUE TO PROTECT THE FUTURE FROM PEOPLE LIKE US.
"LET'S SHOW HIM HOW BADLY HE FAILED."

KATHMANDU
-2 III 33
KN-38 N.D.C.

I FIGURE FORTY GRAND APIECE BY THE END OF THE YEAR.
IF TENZING PULLS UP THEIR RECORDS, IF THE FAMILIES CONSENT, IF WE CAN GET THE BODIES DOWN.
I'M NOT EXACTLY SPENDING IT YET, HASKELL.

HAVE SOME FAITH IN HUMANITY, SUZANNE.
SOMEONE WILL ALWAYS PAY. PEOPLE GET FUNNY ABOUT THEIR DEAD.

PLEASE DON'T TELL ME YOU'RE PLAYING WITH THE HANDS.
NOT PLAYING. LOOKING.
THIS ONE'S ANCIENT.

THE SUMMIT ONE?
IT'S NOT THAT OLD. MAYBE TWENTY YEARS. YOUNG BY EVEREST'S YARDSTICK.
A LONG SHOT THAT ANYONE'S STILL WORRIED ABOUT HIM, BUT HELL, I WAS ALREADY UP THERE.
TIK
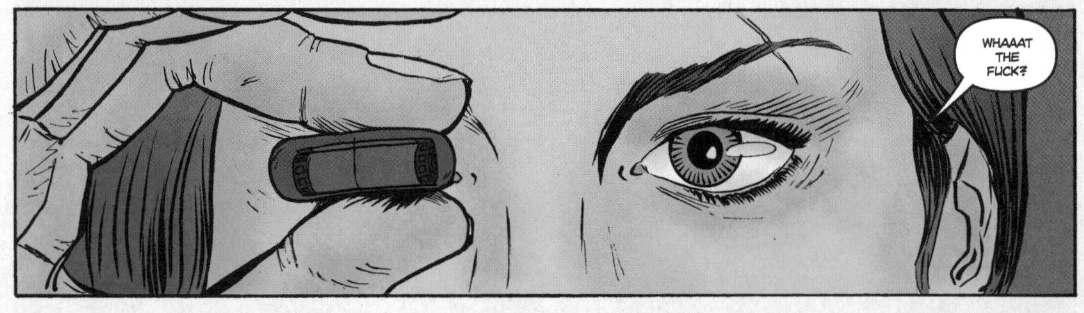
WHAAAT THE FUCK?

HERE, EAT. MAYBE IT'LL SOAK UP THE BOOZE.
AND WE'RE NOT EATING WITH THOSE ON THE TABLE.
PUT 'EM IN THE BANK. BEFORE THEY GO BAD.

I SHOULDN'T *HAVE* TO REMIND YOU, BUT PLEASE WASH YOUR HANDS.
YES, DAD.

OKAY, MYSTERY LIMB...

...LET'S SEE WHO YOU USED TO BE.

HOW MUCH CASH DO YOU HAVE HOARDED AWAY IN THERE ANYWAY?
WHY? YOU NEED A LOAN?
DON'T BE COY, OLD MAN. WHAT DO YOU PLAN TO *DO* WITH IT?
NOTHING. RETIRE.
HA! *YOU?* RETIRED?

NOTHING'S STOPPING YOU. GET OUT WHILE THE GETTING'S GOOD AND ALL THAT.
YOU'RE SITTING ON A SMALL FORTUNE, HASKELL. *USE* IT.
EXACTLY. SMALL. I NEED *MORE*. WHEN I LEAVE, I PLAN TO STAY LEFT.
BESIDES, I'VE GOT A FEW THINGS LEFT TO TAKE CARE OF HERE FIRST.
EVENTUALLY I'M GOING TO IOWA CITY. MY KID LIVES THERE. GONNA BUY A NICE HOUSE, GET TO KNOW MY GRANDKIDS, AND I WON'T CLIMB ANYTHING TALLER THAN A FLIGHT OF STEEP STAIRS EVER AGAIN IF I CAN HELP IT...

SUZANNE?

YOU ASLEEP, SUZANNE?

MMM? NO. I'M AWAKE. SORRY.
IT'S LATE AND YOU'RE WASTED. PLEASE HUMOR ME AND TAKE THE COUCH.
I'M FINE, HASKELL. I'M CERTAINLY NOT WASTED.

"I JUST WANT TO SLEEP IN MY OWN BED. IT'S NOT THAT FAR."
"OKAY, I TRIED. COME BY TOMORROW. I'LL HAVE THE NAMES FROM TENZING. WE CAN START MAKING CALLS."
"MM-HM. BRIGHT AND EARLY.

"HEY, HASKELL?
"DOES IT EVER BOTHER YOU?
"WHAT WE DO?"

"TROUBLED SLEEP, GUILTY THOUGHTS, THAT SORT OF THING?"
"YEAH."
"EVERY NIGHT. BUT NOT BECAUSE OF ANYTHING WE'VE EVER DONE."

Quit my job today.

It didn't go smoothly. It wasn't bound to.
Organizations like mine like to hold on to their heavy hitters until we're too old and useless to come looking for answers.

With any situation, you want to have an exit strategy in case you need to slip out before the world falls in on your head.
I've worked for the government for two decades. I have a dozen plans, fail-safes upon fail-safes, redundancies galore.

In my career, I was whatever the mission required.
A cipher, a multitool, a weapon to point at something and tell it to die.
They never had any idea I would quit, and no idea what I'd do if I ever did.
Me either.

DEPARTURES
East Gates
Time Flight To Status Gate
Freedom is baffling.
Before, I'd get a phone call, a dead drop. I knew where I was going, what I was doing.
Who I was supposed to be.
Being free for the first time? It's awful.
They're coming after me. They'll keep coming until they put me down. All I have left is a bit of insurance and dumb luck.
It's almost a source of comfort.
One way or another, Sullivan Mars has to die.
GOD-DAMMIT!
Message received at 10:24 a.m.
SUZANNE? HASKELL.
GOT THE NAMES FROM TENZING. I'M GOING TO MAKE SOME CALLS. SEE WHAT SHAKES LOOSE.
COME BY WHENEVER YOU MANAGE TO STAGGER OUT OF BED.
Message received at 12:11 p.m.
ZAAAAAAAN!
YOU DITCHED ME MID-DRINKS! ME! LEFT ME LOOKING LIKE A TIT, DEFENDING MY POOR, INVISIBLE FRIEND FROM IMAGINARY STALKERAZZI.
I ENDED UP GOING HOME WITH THE DOUCHE IN THE BEANIE. HIS NAME IS TOLLIVER. CAN YOU STAND IT?
TEXT ME, YOU SHIT.
Message received at 1:24 p.m.
HEY, IT'S DANIEL. YOU COMING BY THE AIR TONIGHT? FIRST ONE'S ON THE HOUSE.
Message received at 1:46 p.m.
TIK-TIK-TIK
CUH-CLICK

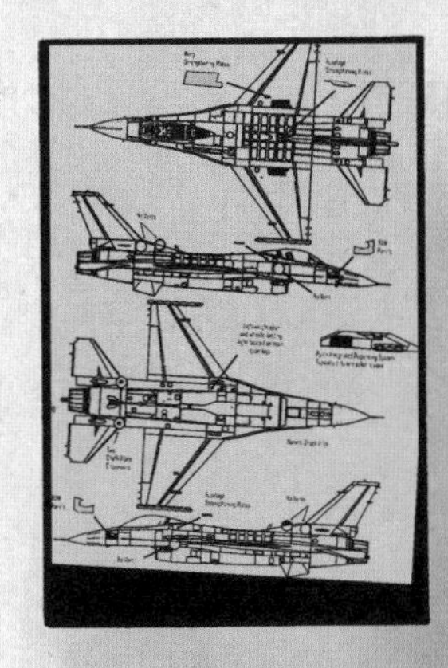

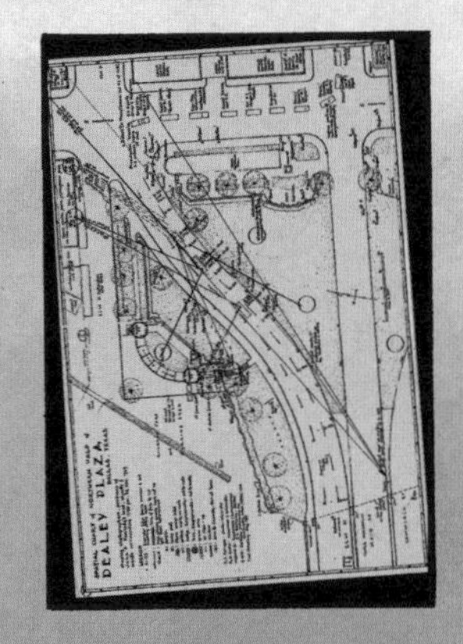

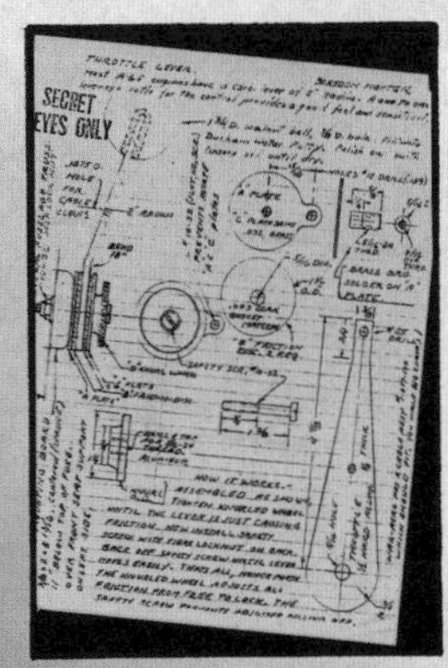

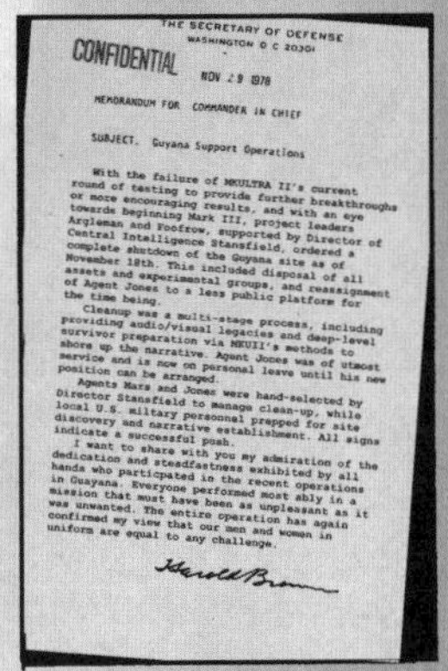

THE SECRETARY OF DEFENSE
WASHINGTON D C 20301

CONFIDENTIAL

NOV 29 1978

MEMORANDUM FOR COMMANDER IN CHIEF

SUBJECT. Guyana Support Operations

With the failure of MKULTRA II's current round of testing to provide further breakthroughs or more encouraging results, and with an eye towards beginning Mark III, project leaders Argleman and Foofrow, supported by Director of Central Intelligence Stansfield, ordered a complete shutdown of the Guyana site as of November 18th. This included disposal of all assets and experimental groups, and reassignment of Agent Jones to a less public platform for the time being.

Cleanup was a multi-stage process, including providing audio/visual legacies and deep-level survivor preparation via MKUII's methods to shore up the narrative. Agent Jones was of utmost service and is now on personal leave until his new position can be arranged.

Agents Mars and Jones were hand-selected by Director Stansfield to manage clean-up, while local U.S. military personnel prepped for site discovery and narrative establishment. All signs indicate a successful push.

I want to share with you my admiration of the dedication and steadfastness exhibited by all hands who participated in the recent operations in Guayana. Everyone performed most ably in a mission that must have been as unpleasant as it was unwanted. The entire operation has again confirmed my view that our men and women in uniform are equal to any challenge.

Harold Brown

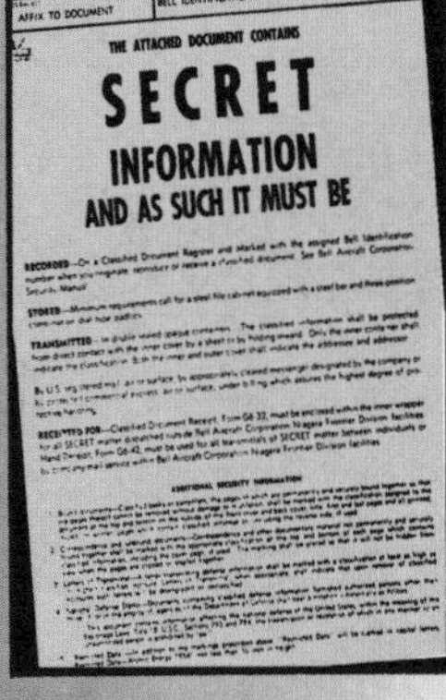

AFFIX TO DOCUMENT | BELL IDENTIFICATION NO

THE ATTACHED DOCUMENT CONTAINS

SECRET

INFORMATION
AND AS SUCH IT MUST BE

RECORDED—On a Classified Document Register and Marked with the assigned Bell Identification number ...

STORED—...

TRANSMITTED—...

RECEIPTED FOR—...

ADDITIONAL SECURITY INFORMATION

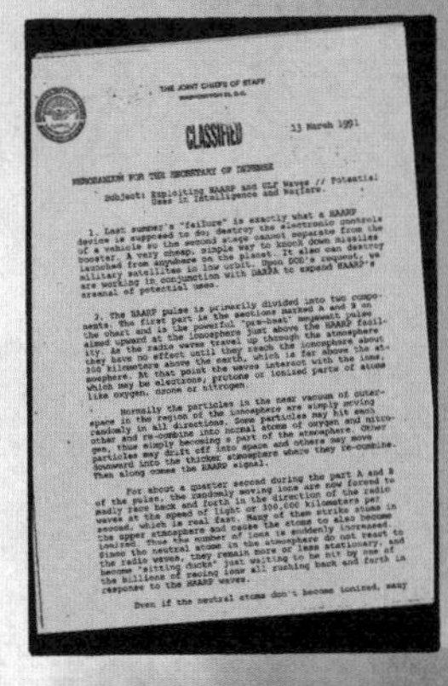

THE JOINT CHIEFS OF STAFF

CLASSIFIED

13 March 1991

MEMORANDUM FOR THE SECRETARY OF DEFENSE

Subject: Exploiting HAARP and ELF Waves // Potential Uses in Intelligence and Warfare.

1. Last summer's "failure" is exactly what a HAARP device is supposed to do; destroy the electronic controls of a vehicle so the second stage cannot separate from the booster. A very cheap, simple way to knock down missiles launched from anywhere on the planet. It also can destroy military satellites in low orbit. Upon DOD's request, we are working in conjunction with DARPA to expand HAARP's arsenal of potential uses.

2. The HAARP pulse is primarily divided into two components. The first part is the sections marked A and B on the chart and is the powerful "pre-heat" megawatt pulse aimed upward at the ionosphere just above the HAARP facility. As the radio waves travel up through the atmosphere they have no effect until they reach the ionosphere about 200 kilometers above the earth, which is far above the atmosphere. At that point the waves interact with the ions, which may be electrons, protons or ionized parts of atoms like oxygen, ozone or nitrogen.

Normally the particles in the near vacuum of outer-space in the region of the ionosphere are simply moving randomly in all directions. Some particles may hit each other and re-combine into normal atoms of oxygen and nitrogen, thus simply becoming a part of the atmosphere. Other particles may drift off into space and others may move downward into the thicker atmosphere where they re-combine. Then along comes the HAARP signal.

For about a quarter second during the part A and B of the pulse, the randomly moving ions are now forced to madly race back and forth in the direction of the radio waves at the speed of light or 300,000 kilometers per second, which is real fast. Many of them strike atoms in the upper atmosphere and cause the atoms to also become ionized. Thus the number of ions is suddenly increased. Since the neutral atoms in the atmosphere do not react to the radio waves, they remain more or less stationary, and become "sitting ducks" just waiting to be hit by one of the billions of racing ions all rushing back and forth in response to the HAARP waves.

Even if the neutral atoms don't become ionized, many

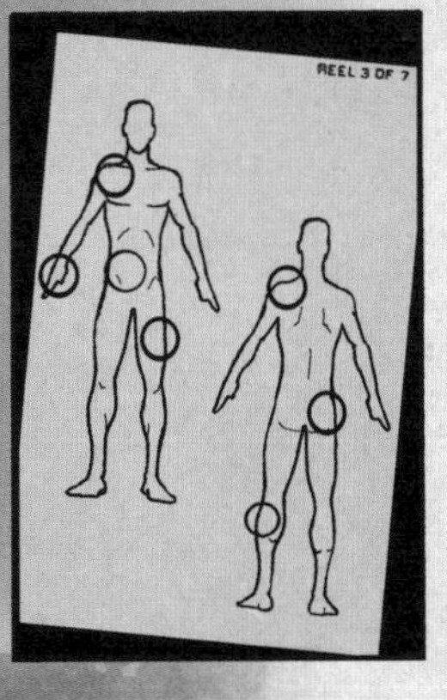

REEL 3 OF 7
I NEED A DRINK.
I DON'T THINK WE SHOULD'VE HAD THAT LAST ROUND.
NONSENSE! THIS IS A *PARTY!* WE MUST KEEP GOING!
SO LONG AS YOU KEEP PAYING.
BAR
करोके
TAXI!
THWOMP!
SCREEEEEEEEEE
TENZING ATAL.
GET IN THE VAN.
WHERE IS SULLIVAN MARS?

SIR, WE HAVE HANDYMEN ON STAFF WHO WOULD BE MORE THAN HAPPY TO FIX YOUR LUGGAGE FOR YOU.
HONESTLY, IT'S AN EASY FIX. HAPPENS EVERY TIME WE GO ON VACATION.
I JUST NEED TO APPLY A LITTLE BRUTE FORCE.
I LOVE THESE FANCY HOTELS. ALL THE COMFORTS OF HOME WHEREVER YOU GO.
AND IF SOMETHING IS MISSING? MAKE A CALL AND THEY BRING IT RIGHT UP TO YOU.
NOW... WHERE WERE WE?
PLEASE, SIR, I DO NOT KNOW WHERE TO FIND THIS MR. MARS YOU'RE LOOKING FOR.
AH, RIGHT.
YOU WERE BEING DIFFICULT.
WHERE IS SULLIVAN MARS?
MR. PRICE... HASKELL PRICE. HE FOUND YOUR MR. MARS.
RUN A LOOKUP, FELLAS.
PLEASE... PLEASE STOP BREAKING MY FINGERS.
IF YOU INSIST.

I SAID I'D BUY YOU A ROUND. DIDN'T MEAN A WHOLE BOTTLE.
PLUS I SORTA ASSUMED WE'D HANG OUT. NOT YOU HIDING IN THE CORNER.
DANNY, PLEASE. NOT RIGHT NOW.
OH, I SEE. TONIGHT THEN? CLOSING TIME, MY PLACE?
FINE. PERFECT. NOW GO AWAY.
BRING THE BOTTLE HOME WITH YOU.
I LIKE YOUR HAIR DOWN LIKE THAT, ZAN.
I grew up dirt poor, joined the army, went to Vietnam. I killed a lot of people like Uncle Sam asked me to.
I didn't realize I was so good at it until some feds in black suits and shiny wingtips invited me out to dinner in Saigon.
"Do you want a job?" they asked.
They gave me a license for chaos.
I killed bad guys, I stole state secrets, I blew big, important things up. We got ricin umbrellas, reverse handguns, and big expense accounts.
Learned new languages, saw the world, and got paid offensive amounts of money to do it all.
I was special. Strange Agents, they called us, the kind other spooks shy away from.
For a long time, it was a perfect life.
Why did I quit again?
Well, it starts with me killing someone.
Most of my stories start that way.

BZZZT
BZZZT
BZZZT
BEET-DEET

GOD. CALM ***DOWN***, HASKELL. I'M COMING.
HASKELL PRICE
5 MISSED CALLS

CHEMICALLY, IT'S HARD TO BE DRUNK ***AND*** SCARED. I SHOULD BE FEELING FANCY FUCKING FREE.
BUT ALL I CAN THINK OF IS THIS ROLL OF FILM IN MY SWEATY HAND, THIS CRAZY MAN'S DIARY.

IT'S ALL NONSENSE UNTIL YOU STOP TO CONSIDER ITS... WHAT DO THEY CALL IT?
PROVENANCE.
TWENTY YEARS ON TOP OF MT. EVEREST IN A DEAD MAN'S HAND. ***THAT*** AFFIRMS MY FAITH.
SOMETHING LIKE THIS IS WORTH A ***LOT*** OF MONEY TO SOMEONE. AND A LOT OF BAD NEWS TO EVERYONE ELSE.

HASKELL WILL--
...SO THEN YOU GO LEFT AND HEAD ***29,000*** FEET STRAIGHT UP MY ***ASS***, YOU SONUV--
ARGHHH!
VERTEBRAE OR JOKES, MR. PRICE--WHICH WILL GIVE OUT FIRST?
WHERE. IS. SULLIVAN. ***MARS?***
ST-STACKED IN MY FR-FREEZER, BABY G-GENIUS.

OKAY, MY TURN NOW.
I'VE BEEN HOPING WE'D GET TO THIS PART OF THE EVENING BEFORE TOO LONG.
IT GETS BORING, JUST STUDYING THIS STUFF.
YOU HAVE NO IDEA HOW MANY OF THESE THINGS I'VE GOT IN MY HEAD, ALL ITCHING TO GET LOOSE.
THIS ONE, IT'S AN OLDIE BUT A GOODIE.
FAIR WARNING, THIS IS GOING TO BE A BIT MESSY. AND VERY PAINFUL.
PLUS WE HAVE TO KILL THE RAT AFTERWARDS AND ALL.
POOR THING'LL BE PRETTY MUCH INSANE BY THE TIME IT EATS THROUGH YOUR STOMACH.

ENOUGH PRELUDE.

WE'RE HERE TO STEAL YOUR SECRETS.
REVEAL THEM IN ANY ORDER YOU PREFER.

EITHER WE CRACK YOU OPEN OR OUR FRIEND UNDER GLASS DOES.
SIMPLE MATH.
WHERE IS SULLIVAN MARS?
GRAAAArrGK

STUPID BACKWARDS NON-911-HAVING ASSHOLE COUNTRY.

THANK YOU FOR JOINING US, MISS JENSEN.
WE ARE AGENTS IN PURSUIT OF A DANGEROUS FUGITIVE.
KK...
AND THIS IS A LARYNGEAL CHOKE. IT'S WHY YOU CAN'T SEEM TO SCREAM.
NOW. WOULD YOU JOIN US INSIDE, WHERE IT'S A TAD MORE PRIVATE?

KLAK!

GENTLEMEN! SAY HELLO TO MISS ZAN--
RAAAAHHRR

WHEN I SLEEP...
I'M A FALLING STAR...
STRAY DOG!
I CAN TASTE THE GLORY ESCAPING THROUGH MY BLOODY LIPS.

WHEN I WAKE UP, I'M SPACE JUNK, AN OBJECT LESSON...
A HAS-BEEN IN HIDING FROM ENEMIES CREATED AND IMAGINED.

RIGHT THIS VERY MOMENT, LIFE IS SIMPLER THAN IT'S EVER BEEN.
TAXI
I'M ALIVE.
ALL I HAVE TO DO IS STAY THAT WAY.

TOP SECRET
THE JOINT CHIEFS OF STAFF
WASHINGTON 25, D.C.
ARY OF DEFENSE

SOME HELPFUL HINTS WHEN BEING PURSUED:
BREATHE.

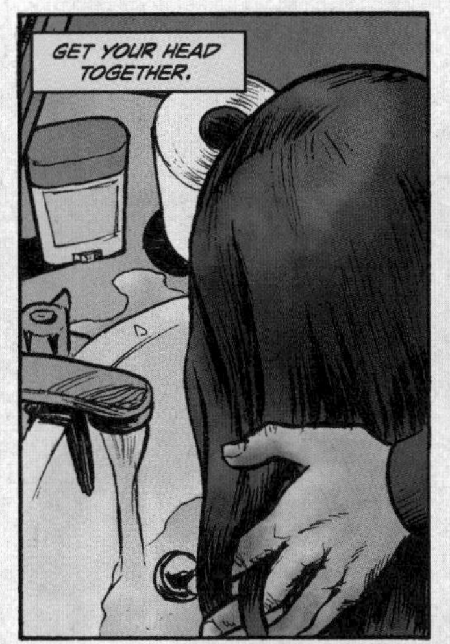
GET YOUR HEAD TOGETHER.

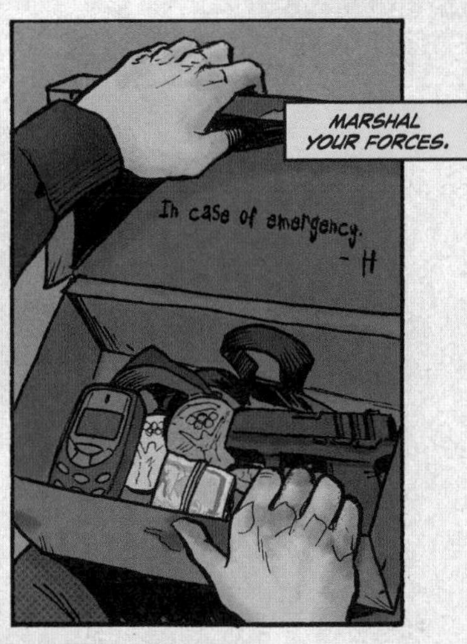
MARSHAL YOUR FORCES.
In case of emergency.
- H

STAY CALM.

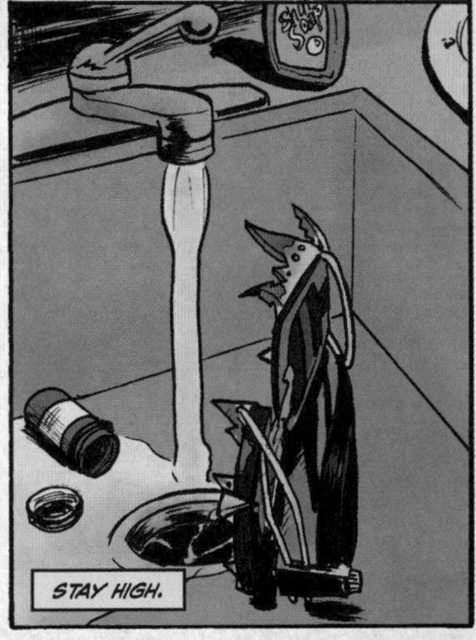
STAY HIGH.

THE PAST IS LUGGAGE.

PICK YOUR ESCAPE ROUTE.

AND WHEN THINGS GO SIDEWAYS...
...AND THEY ALWAYS WILL...

BE READY TO RUN.

I'M GOOD AT RUNNING.
AFTER THE CRASH, I HAD AN ARMY OF PRESS, LAWYERS, I.O.C. OFFICIALS, AND COPS AFTER ME.
TRYING TO TAKE EVERYTHING I'D WORKED FOR.

THESE ARE JUST THREE GUYS IN TAILORED SUITS.

THEY JUST WANT MY LIFE.

WHEN THEY ASK FOR YOUR MEDALS BACK, IT'S ALL VERY CIVILIZED.
A CERTIFIED LETTER. A SOFT DEADLINE.
P-KSSH

PLENTY OF TIME TO MULL OVER YOUR OPTIONS.
TO TRY TO FIGURE OUT WHO YOU'LL BE NOW.

I DID MY HOMEWORK. EMPTIED THE ACCOUNTS I COULD. 3 A.M. FLIGHT, CASH ONLY. NO NOTES.
STASHED THE MEDALS IN MY CHECK-IN BAG.

TWO SUITCASES TO FIT A WHOLE LIFE IN.
I COULD BARELY MANAGE TO FILL ONE.
BUT I WAS FREE. I COULD BUY MYSELF A NEW LIFE.

NO MORE WATCHERS. NO MORE TRAINING. NO MORE LOSING.
WHAT COULD POSSIBLY GO WRONG?

FIRST I BURNED MY WAY THROUGH EUROPE.
LIVING OUT ALL THOSE TEENAGE FANTASIES LOST TO A RIGOROUSLY SCHEDULED LIFE.
THINK. THINK. FUCK.
IT GETS A BIT SORDID, THE BITS I REMEMBER.

THEN CAME ASIA, RECOVERY. WHERE ENLIGHTENMENT OVERTOOK HEDONISM.
IN DIRECT RELATION TO MY DWINDLING BANK BALANCE.

I GOT TO KATHMANDU AND STOPPED. EXHAUSTED OR DESTINED, IT FELT RIGHT.
THANK YOU.
ALL THOSE PEAKS EAGER TO BE CLIMBED.
JUST ME AND THEM. NOTHING COULD INTERFERE.

HOME AT LAST.
NO MORE RUNNING, I TOLD MYSELF.
I'M SUCH A FUCKING IDIOT SOMETIMES.

ANYONE GOT EYES ON HER?
PFFFSST

NEGATIVE.

THEY'RE ROUNDING US UP.
EASY, BOY. STAY.
AT LEAST YOU'RE SACRED.
YOU STAND A WAY BETTER CHANCE THAN ME.

ALL THAT'S LEFT IS ME.

PFFFSST
PFFFSST
PFFFSST

ME AND SULLIVAN.
NINE-TENTHS OF WHOM IS BURIED ON TOP OF EVEREST.

MIGHT AS WELL BE THE MOON...

...BECAUSE WHY SHOULD ANYTHING EVER BE EASY?
GRAB THE PACK. GET THE MEDALS. EMPTY THE KIT.
GRAB THE PACK. GET THE MEDALS. EMPTY THE KIT.

GET THE MEDALS. EMPTY THE KIT. GET THE MEDALS. EMPTY THE KIT.
MOVE.

STAY.
UHFF

MISS JENSEN.
CAN YOU FEEL IT? THAT DARKNESS CREEPING IN ON THE EDGES?
THAT'S MY FAVORITE PART.
I CAN MAKE IT LAST FOR HOURS.
COMPARED TO MY FELLOW MONSTERS OUT THERE LOOKING FOR YOU, THIS IS A MERCY.
JUST LET IT HAPPEN. WE'VE GOT TIMETABLES TO KEEP TO.
OR ANSWER THE QUESTION OF THE HOUR.
WHERE IS SULLIVAN MARS?
"I DON'T KNOW."

OKAY. THEN DO YOU HAVE SOME IDEA WHEN YOU'RE COMING *OUT?*

OR DID YOU JUST BURST IN HERE TO SHOOT UP IN MY BATHROOM?
FUCK *OFF*, DANIEL.

JESUS. LOVELY TALK.
YOU SHOW UP LATE, DRUNK AS A PRIEST, HIGH AS A KITE.
WHICH, GRANTED, I'M *USED* TO.
LOOKING LIKE SOMEONE KICKED THE SHIT OUT OF YOU. FINE. I WON'T ASK ABOUT THAT EITHER.
WHAT EXACTLY AM I *SUPPOSED* TO DO?

NOTHING. SAME AS ALWAYS.
WHY ELSE DO YOU THINK WE GET ALONG SO WELL?

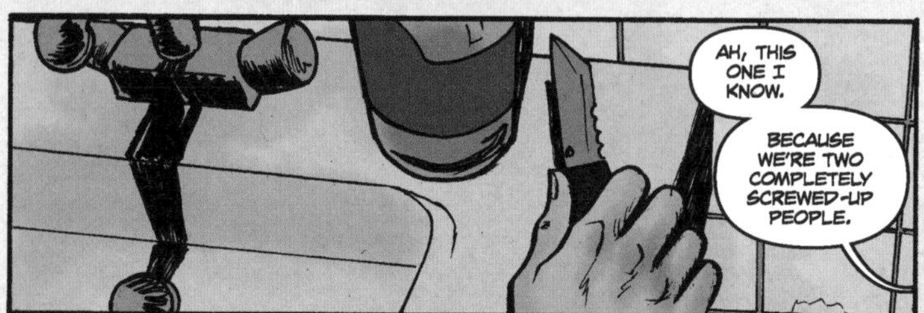
AH, THIS ONE I KNOW.
BECAUSE WE'RE TWO COMPLETELY SCREWED-UP PEOPLE.

WHAT'S WITH THE PACK, ZAN?

RIGHT. THAT.
I'VE GOT ANOTHER GIG WITH TALL TALES.
ANOTHER RICH ASSHOLE WITH A TROPHY FIXATION.
I WON'T BE AROUND FOR A BIT.
RIGHT. SAME AS ALWAYS.

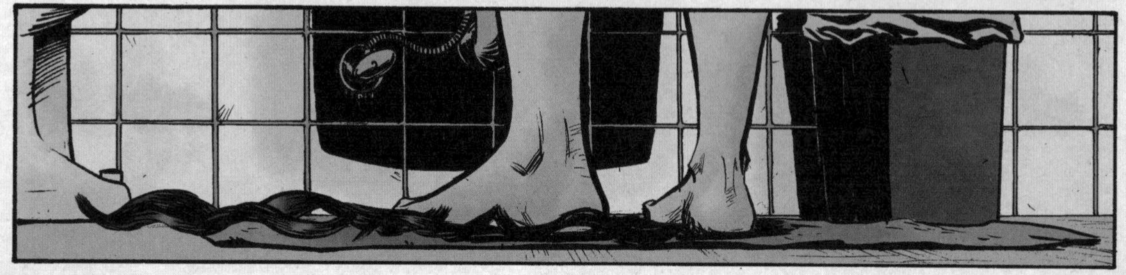

SHH. IT'S OKAY, ZAN. WHATEVER IT IS, WE'LL FIX IT.
THIS'LL ALL LOOK BETTER BY MORNING. SWEAR.

BZZZT BZZZT BZZZT
AUTOMATIC.
PAVLOVIAN.
I PRESS ANSWER WITHOUT THINKING.
BEEP
THE ONLY ONE WHO HAS THIS NUMBER IS HASKELL.
HE GAVE ME THE PHONE WHEN HE GAVE ME THE GUN AND A WAD OF CASH.
"JUST IN CASE."

H-HASKELL?
NO, ZAN.
SORRY TO BE SO INFORMAL. INTERESTING FILE YOU'VE GOT.
I THINK I SAW YOU ON T.V. ONCE. WHAT *HAPPENED?*
TOO MUCH PRESSURE? A LOT OF PEOPLE CRACK UNDER THE LEAST--
WHERE'S HASKELL?
DON'T WORRY. WE'RE TAKING CARE OF THE OLD MAN.
NOW DO YOU WANT TO HEAR THE GOOD NEWS OR THE BAD?
ENGLISH AIR

JUST KIDDING, IT'S ALL BAD NEWS.
EXCEPT FOR YOU. COMMENDABLE BEHAVIOR OUT IN THE FIELD, ZAN.
THOUGH YOU DO HAVE HOME FIELD ADVANTAGE. BUT STILL, WELL DONE.
YOU'RE THE BRIGHT SPOT IN AN OTHERWISE-LACKING ASSIGNMENT.
SHAME ABOUT WHAT WE HAVE TO DO TO YOU.
WE'RE CALLING TO LET YOU KNOW WE CAN FIND YOU.
THAT WE'RE COMING BACK FOR YOU.
ONCE WE RETRIEVE MR. MARS, OF COURSE.
YOUR PARTNER FINALLY CAME AROUND. TOLD US EVERYTHING WE NEEDED.

THOUGH IT TOOK SOME CONVINCING.

HE'S EVEN KINDLY AGREED TO LEAD THE WAY THERE.

OH!
ALMOST FORGOT!

WE LEFT YOU A LITTLE GIFT IN MR. PRICE'S FREEZER.
COMING ATTRACTIONS, IF YOU WILL.
HOPE YOU LIKE IT.

THE HELL ARE YOU DOING, OVER THERE, MISTER?
HEY!
MORNING! WOULD YOU BELIEVE HE OWES ME MONEY?
WANT TO HELP ME COLLECT IT?
WHAT?
ARE YOU SERIOUSLY LOOTING BODIES?
NAW, I'M SAVING THEM. BRINGING 'EM HOME.
"YOU WANT TO HELP? YOU LOOK LIKE YOU COULD DO WITH A BIT OF GOOD KARMA."
"I PROBABLY COULD.
"WHAT DOES IT PAY?"

DANIEL?
YOU AWAKE?

MM? I THINK SO.
WHAT HAPPENED TO YOU?
YOU LOOK... NORMAL.
THANKS?
I FOUND CONCEALER IN YOUR BATHROOM.
GUESSING IT DOESN'T BELONG TO YOU.
I CAN EXPLAIN THAT.
NO TIME. DOESN'T MATTER.
THIS IS FAREWELL THEN?
IT'S A BUSINESS TRIP, DANIEL. I'LL BE BACK IN A--
C'MON, ZAN. CAN WE SKIP THE LIES?
YOU'RE GOING HOME, RIGHT?
HOME HOME.
NO... I'M...
HOW DID YOU KNOW?
"JUST BEEN PAYING ATTENTION IS ALL."
"I HATE THAT ABOUT YOU.
"BYE, DANIEL. MAYBE..."
THERE SHE IS. ABANDONER OF FRIENDS. ASKER OF CRAP FAVORS AT UNGODLY HOURS.
AND OH MY *GOD*, HAIRCUT! MAKEUP! WHAT DID YOU DO WITH ZAN?
YOUR BOYFRIEND'S STARING AT US.
CAN WE *GO*, SOPHIE?
RIGHT. MAYBE.

MOVE IT, ARSEHOLE!
WE'VE GOT *PLACES* TO BE.

WHERE'S IT *THIS* TIME, ZAN? PANGA BUBSY OR SOME SUCH?
Tribhuvan Int'l Airport
FURTHER THAN THAT.

WELL, FIRST DRINK'S ON ME WHEN YOU GET BACK.
'KAY. I'D LIKE THAT.

YOU KNOW I WORRY ABOUT YOU, GIRL.
PEOPLE *DIE* UP THERE, EVEN PROS LIKE YOU.
DO ME A FAVOR? DON'T DIE?

DEPARTURES
I'LL DO MY BEST.
DON'T GO TURNING ALL *NICE* WHILE I'M GONE.
NEVER.

TAKE CARE OF YOURSELF, ZAN.
REMEMBER, YOU PROMISED TO COME BACK FOR THAT DRINK.
DON'T THINK I PROMISED.
LET'S PRETEND YOU DID.

DEPARTURES
FLIGHT TIME DESTINATION STATUS GATE
UA5207 7:00 MADRID DEPARTING 45
CP889 7:00 HONG KONG BOARDING 27
AF043 7:15 PARIS ON TIME 19
BA7368 7:40 LONDON ON TIME 33
AL822 8:00 MEL DELAYED 56
CP889 8:20 LE ON TIME 11
"LOVE YOU, SOPHIE."
"LOVE YOU TOO. DON'T GET LOST. I'M NOT PAYING *HASKELL* TO BRING YOUR BODY HOME."

I CAN'T BELIEVE I'M LEAVING.
WITHOUT EVEREST. WITHOUT HASKELL. JESUS. STOP. STOP THINKING ABOUT IT.
LICE OFFICER IN KATHM
AA
ericanAirlines
GET HOME. YOU CAN USE THIS MICROFILM, BUY YOURSELF AND HASKELL A WAY OUT.
MAYBE EVEN BUY YOUR OLD LIFE BACK. IF THEY WANT IT, THEY'LL PAY FOR IT.

SGRACED OLYMPIC GOLD MEDALIST SOUGHT IN CONNECTION WITH HOMIC
IT'S NOT LIKE THEY CAN STOP ME NOW.
IT'S...NO. NO NO NO NO NO NO.

GET YOUR HEAD TOGETHER.

MARSHAL YOUR FORCES.
STAY CALM.

STAY HIGH.
YOU'RE ALMOST BROKE. ALL ALONE. CAN'T GO HOME; OR BACK TO KATHMANDU.
AND THE BLACK-FLANNEL ASSHOLES RESPONSIBLE ARE ON THEIR WAY TO EVEREST.
EVEREST. THERE'S AN OPTION.
MAYBE IT COULD FIX EVERYTHING.
SAVE HASKELL, LOOT MARS'S BODY, REACH THE SUMMIT.
WALK OVER THE MOUNTAIN. RIGHT INTO CHINA. DISAPPEAR.
IT'S PERFECT.

AH! YOU'RE IN LUCK.
THAT'S A FIRST.
WE HAVE A FEW SEATS ON THE NEXT CHARTER TO LUKLA.
LEAVING IN...20 MINUTES.
AWESOME. LET'S DO THIS.
EXCUSE ME, BUT ARE YOU OKAY, MISS?
ME? I'M FABULOUS. WHY?
PARDON ME. I DIDN'T MEAN ANYTHING. JUST. ALL...THIS?
HA HA, OH, IT'S NOTHING. CLIMBING MISHAP. FELL DOWN A PEAK.
WOW. WELL, DOESN'T SEEM LIKE IT'S SLOWED YOU DOWN.
YOU'RE HEADING TO EVEREST? LIKE, ALL THE WAY?
YEP.
YOU MUST BE SO EXCITED.
आगमन ARRIVAL
"YOU'D THINK SO, WOULDN'T YOU?"

The world's a small place.
HEY, YOU GOING TO EVEREST TOO?
WHAT ARE YOU READING?
Smaller when you're trying to run from it.
I've planned for that too.

"Past behavior predicts future behavior." The Agency taught us that.
With every target I ever tracked down, it's become the rare breed of truth that persists.
So I'm retreating, back beyond the training and the tests. Back before they could track me.
Back to that dumbass farm kid, watching the horizon, dreaming of anywhere else.

GOOD. EVERYTHING WILL BE WAITING FOR YOU, AGENT.
LISTEN, I DON'T CARE IF YOU FIREBOMB EVERY INCH OF THAT ROCK, I WANT MARS BACK HERE.
THEN YOU'D BETTER STAY UP THERE. AND HOPE GOD REACHES YOU BEFORE I DO.
Biratnagar
Back when I wasn't scared of dying.
Just scared of it not counting for something.
It's kind of nice, letting go of free will. Letting predestination take over.
All roads ahead are blocked. There's only one route left open.
As high and as far away as I can go.

KATHMANDU

[illegible] at the
[illegible]YAL NEPALESE EMBASSY
New Delhi

Type of Visa.............................. [illegible]
No. Date
Good for single journey (s)
to the kingdom of Nepal within
three month of date hereof and
stay for 30days from the date of
entry provides the passport remains
Valid.
Fee Rs. 45/- (Forty Five only)

I can't stop thinking about Paris lately.
I used to love that city. It was like going back in time.
Until it caught up with the future.
The great destroyer.
Not that the past is truly any better.
Not that I remember enough of it to say for sure.
Still, some memories always burn bright.
Like your first day.
DON'T GO BACK, MARS.
Or your last.
And all the terrible things you did in between.
The itchy phantom limb of who you're pretending not to be.
TN 0904
I know. You can't leave everything behind.
But goddamn, I've had fun trying.

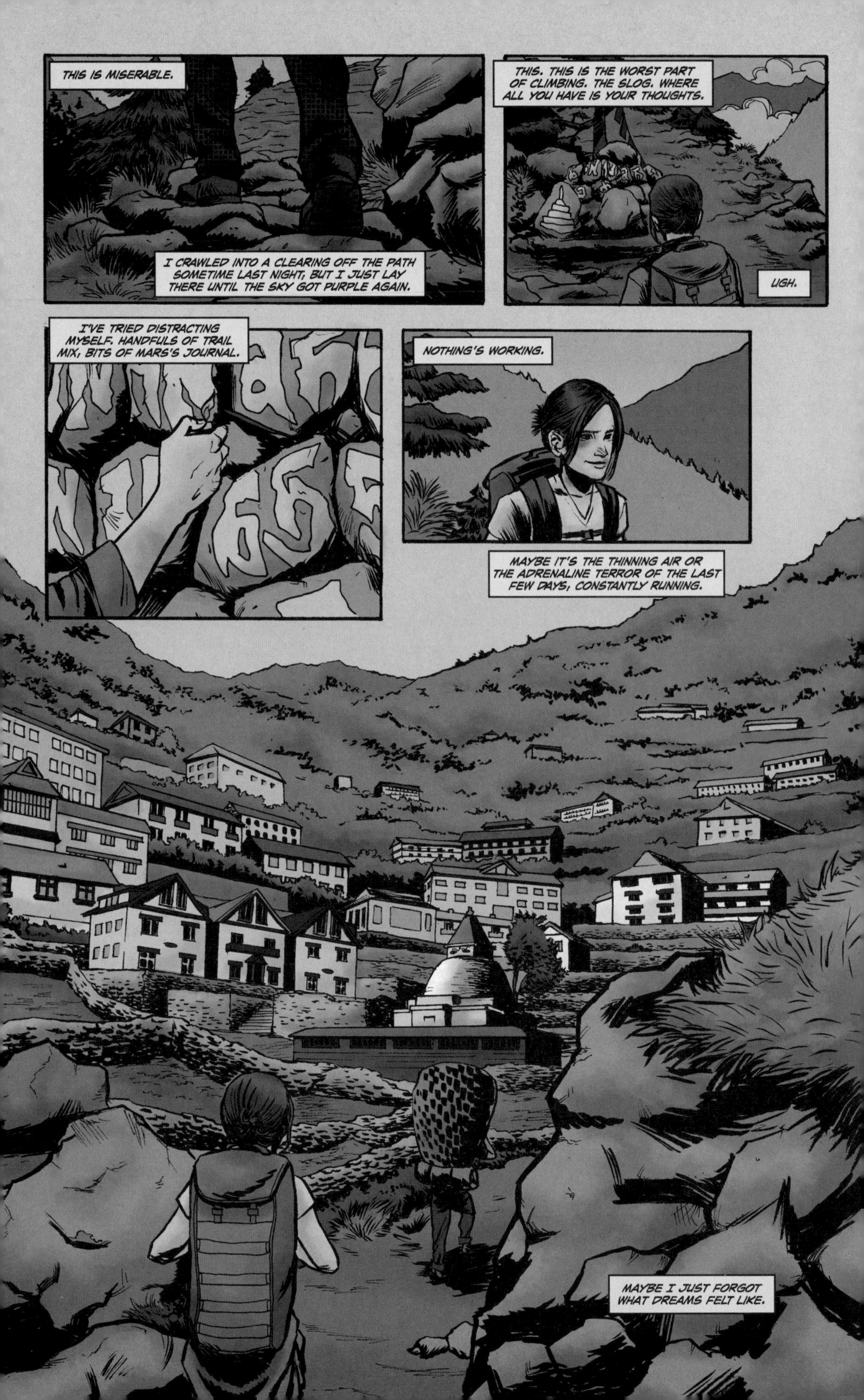
THIS IS MISERABLE.
I CRAWLED INTO A CLEARING OFF THE PATH SOMETIME LAST NIGHT, BUT I JUST LAY THERE UNTIL THE SKY GOT PURPLE AGAIN.
THIS. THIS IS THE WORST PART OF CLIMBING. THE SLOG. WHERE ALL YOU HAVE IS YOUR THOUGHTS.
UGH.
I'VE TRIED DISTRACTING MYSELF. HANDFULS OF TRAIL MIX, BITS OF MARS'S JOURNAL.
NOTHING'S WORKING.
MAYBE IT'S THE THINNING AIR OR THE ADRENALINE TERROR OF THE LAST FEW DAYS, CONSTANTLY RUNNING.
MAYBE I JUST FORGOT WHAT DREAMS FELT LIKE.

NAMCHE BAZAAR.
11,286 FT. ABOVE SEA LEVEL.
ZAN?
WHAT THE HELL ARE YOU DOING?
EATING. WAITING FOR YOU.
NICE TO SEE YOU *TOO*, DORJE.
I MEANT HERE. *NAMCHE*. YOU CAME TO MY *HOUSE*. HOW DO YOU EVEN KNOW WHERE I LIVE?
TALL TALES?
WHEN WE CLIMBED NANGA LAST MONTH?
I'VE STILL GOT THE CONTACT SHEET.
Y'KNOW, IN CASE WE DIED.
AH. TALL TALES, ALWAYS LOOKING OUT FOR US.
YOU ON THE OUTS WITH THEM AGAIN?
YOU WORK FOR THEM. WHAT DO YOU THINK?
I THINK I SORTA QUIT A FEW DAYS AGO.
SO NOW IT LOOKS LIKE WE'RE BOTH FREE.
WHICH IS WHY I'M HERE.
HERE WE GO.
THE MYSTERIOUS OFFER.
REMEMBER THAT TALK WE HAD? ABOUT EVEREST?

...AND WE'D HAVE TO LEAVE SOON.
HOW SOON?
TOMORROW. NEXT DAY AT THE LATEST.
NO PREP, NO MONEY, NO ASSISTANCE?
NO ONE HOLDING US BACK.
ZAN, SUMMITING TAKES WEEKS TO DO. ACCLIMATIZING, REST DAYS, WEATHER WINDOWS.
THAT'S HOW LONG IT TAKES THEM, DORJE.
THEY'RE RUNNING A BUSINESS.
TRYING TO GET RICH DIPSHITS UP TO THE TOP WITHOUT A LAWSUIT.
WE CAN CLIMB IN OUR SLEEP.
WE WON'T HAVE ANYONE DRAGGING US DOWN.
WE'RE USED TO BEING AT ALTITUDE.
YOU, ME, THE MOUNTAIN. IT'S PURE, DORJE. THE WAY IT SHOULD BE.
UH-HUH.
WHY ME?
HOW CLOSE DID YOU GET LAST TIME?
CAMP IV.
JIM MADE ME STAY BEHIND. TO MAKE TEA FOR THE VICTORIOUS CLIMBERS ON THEIR WAY BACK DOWN.
THAT'S WHY.
PLUS YOU DON'T KNOW ANY OTHER SHERPAS.
THAT MONEY'S BURNED, ZAN.
HERE'S A DOWN PAYMENT.
THAT TOO.
NO, IT'S SINGED. IT STILL SPENDS.
DO YOU HAVE MORE?

"YEAH. WHY?"
"WE NEED TO GO SHOPPING.
"YOU PICKED THE LAST CHANCE BEFORE EVEREST TO STOCK UP, SO IT'S GOING TO BE EXPENSIVE.
"MINUS THE HANDY SHERPA DISCOUNT."
"RIGHT THERE. THAT'S WHY I LOVE YOU."

SERIOUSLY, DID YOU NOT PACK AT ALL?
I WAS IN A HURRY.
DO I WANT TO KNOW WHY?
NOT REALLY.

WE'RE CLIMBING TOGETHER, ZAN.
I HAVE TO TRUST YOU.
THEN TRUST ME, DORJE.
ME AND WHAT I'M PAYING YOU.

WHERE ARE YOU STAYING?
CAN YOU TELL ME THAT?
NO. NOWHERE YET.
THEN LET'S GO.
I'M NOT KEEPING THIS IN MY PLACE.

I DON'T WANT TO STAY ANYWHERE TOURISTY.
IT'S NAMCHE. IT'S ALL TOURISTY.
BUT THIS IS WRETCHED ENOUGH TO SUIT YOUR NEEDS.

WE'RE MISSING A FEW THINGS. BIG THINGS.
LOTS OF STUFF THEY DON'T SELL AT THE MARKET.
I KNOW SOMEONE YOU CAN TALK TO.

"I'LL BE BY EARLY. GET SOME SLEEP."
NOT FUCKING LIKELY.
Protocol says to clear the scene within an hour. Every hour beyond that, you put yourself at risk.
But I'd just killed a good friend. Maybe the last one I had left.
I deserved a party.

A girl. A chance to wear the tux I packed. An expense account eager to be abused.
Sleeping in a strange room, roommates whispering in the hallway. It felt like falling back in time.
Throw in drinking and that 3 a.m. notion that you're going to live forever and...
If I broke protocol by staying, I was pissing all over its mangled corpse by doing what I did next.

Call me an unsatisfied employee.

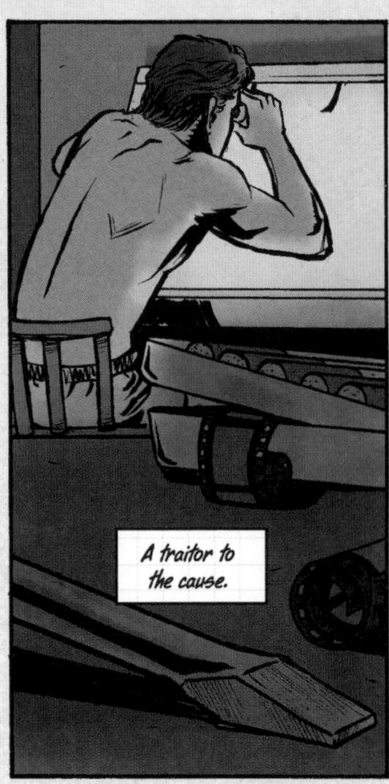
A traitor to the cause.

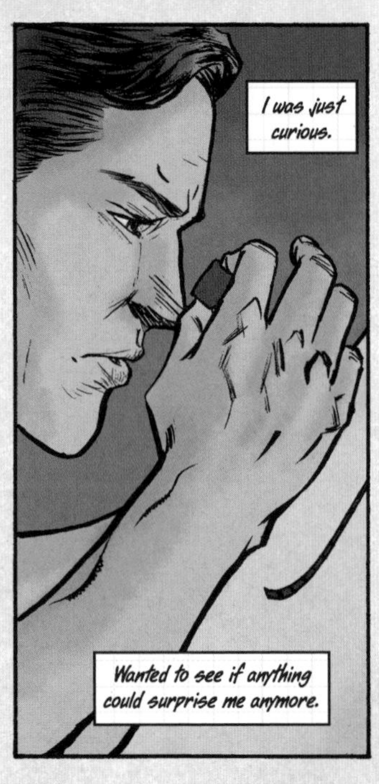
I was just curious.
Wanted to see if anything could surprise me anymore.

Be careful what you wish for.

Our handlers ~~keep~~ kept us isolated for a reason.
In their minds, lives are a series of little boxes.

Separate and neat.
100
196586

This is the problem with being a real person.
Everything gets all mixed up together.
Choices can't be made in a vacuum.

All that stupid history and character getting in the way.
Maybe I should have kept on the regimen.

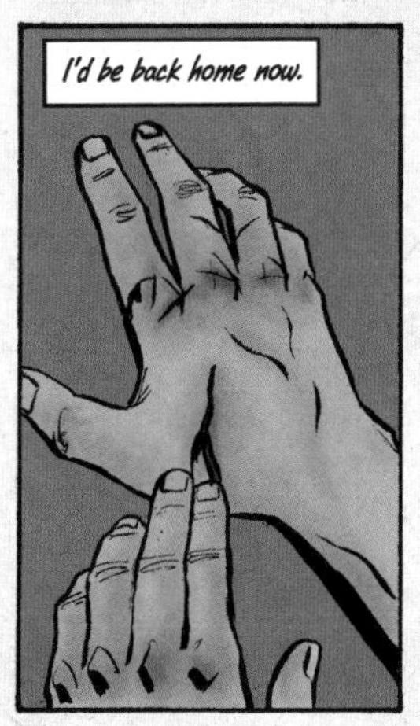
I'd be back home now.

Waiting for them to plug a new program in.

No big changes, no hard decisions.

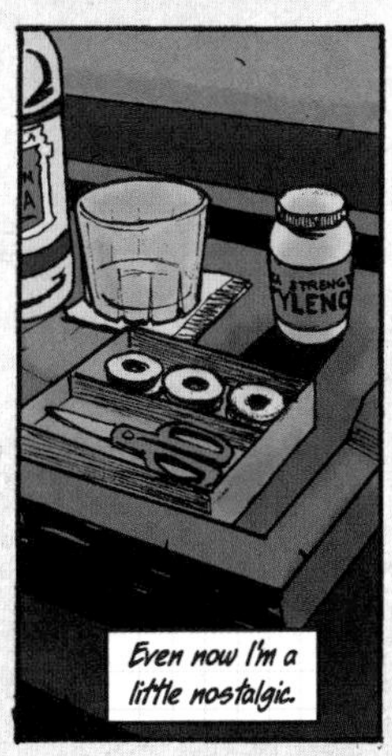
Even now I'm a little nostalgic.

FWUMP
FWUMP
FWUMP
OPEN *UP!*
FWUMP
FWUMP
FWUMP

FWUMP
FWUMP

YOU STILL ASLEEP? IT'S *NOON*.
DON'T WORRY. I WON'T ASK.
LET'S GO. AISHMA'S WAITING.
WHO'S AISHMA?

THERE'S TWO THINGS TO BE AFRAID OF IN NAMCHE.
ONE IS HAVING TO LIVE IN NAMCHE.
THE OTHER IS AISHMA.

ZAN, MEET AISHMA. SHE'S A TRAVELING SALESWOMAN.
YES, YES. I DO NOT HAVE FOREVER.
DORJE STAYS OUT HERE.
PAYING CUSTOMERS ONLY.

HEY, WE'RE NEIGHBORS.
PLEASE. I ONLY *SELL* HERE.
I TRUST YOU'VE BEEN TOLD ABOUT MY PRICES?

"EXORBITANT?"
"GOOD, THAT IS OUT OF THE WAY.
"COME SEE."

"FOUR HIGH-CAPACITY OXYGEN TANKS. RESPIRATOR. KNIVES. FIRST AID. PHARMACEUTICALS. IS THAT ALL?
"AND A CLIMBING PERMIT."
"THIS WILL NOT COVER IT."
"THIS IS ALL I HAVE."
"THAT IS NOT MY PROBLEM."

THESE WERE HARD ENOUGH TO ACQUIRE.
A FALSIFIED PERMIT IS A MIRACLE. AN ILLEGAL ONE.

NO MORE ILLEGAL THAN YOUR INVENTORY.
THESE TANKS? CUSTOM MADE FOR HIGH-END EXPEDITION TEAMS.
YOU CAN'T BUY THEM, NOT EVEN IN KATHMANDU.

THINGS HAVE A WAY OF GETTING LOST ON EVEREST.
CLIMBERS DIE. LOSE TRACK OF THEIR THINGS.
MY EMPLOYEES FIND THESE ITEMS. BRING THEM TO ME.

"AND YOU PEOPLE BARGE THROUGH THE KHUMBU EVERY YEAR, AS IF NOTHING WERE MORE IMPORTANT THAN YOUR OWN GLORY.
YOU DESPOIL OUR MOTHER GODDESS, LEAVE YOUR CORPSES AND TRASH TO ROT ON HER SIDES. AND YOU COMPLAIN WHERE YOUR CRUTCHES COME FROM?"

IT'S NOT THEFT.
CONSIDER IT A SMALL MEASURE OF DIVINE RETRIBUTION.
I AM ANOTHER. YOUR JUDGMENTS ARE LOST ON ME.

BELIEVE ME, AISHMA.
I GOT NO ROOM TO JUDGE. NOT EVEN YOU.
HERE.

WILL THIS COVER THE REST?
YOU DON'T NEED IT?
NOT ANYMORE.
PASSPORT

GOOD LUCK.
GOT 'EM.
WHAT?
DROP IT IN YOUR ROOM. YOU CAN LEAVE YOUR *GUN* BEHIND TOO.
I'LL BE OUTSIDE. WE HAVE TO TALK.

BLACK EYE, A GUN, RACING UP EVEREST ON EMPTY-- EVERYTHING ABOUT YOU SCREAMS, "I AM TROUBLE."
I'M NOT A DUMB PACK MULE, ZAN.
LEVEL WITH ME. TELL ME ANYTHING TO REASSURE ME.
OR I WALK.
NO.

YOU DON'T *GET* TO TELL ME WHAT TO DO. YOU DON'T ORDER ME AROUND.
I MADE YOU AN OFFER, PAID YOU, EQUAL PARTNERS, ONE GOAL.
WE SUMMIT TOGETHER. IF YOU WANT TO BACK OUT, GO. IF YOU WANT TO CLIMB WITH ME, LET'S DO IT.
Come in we

I'LL GO ALONE. CARRY EVERYTHING MYSELF. DIE IF I...
I JUST... I DON'T CARE ANYMORE, DORJE. I CAN'T.

C'MON. YOU'RE GOING TO MAKE ME FEEL BAD.
SO'S THAT A YES?
CALL IT A MAYBE.

I'M LEAVING AT DAYBREAK. IF YOU'RE STILL INTERESTED, MEET ME ON THE TRAIL OUT.
NO.
LEAVE EARLIER. 2 A.M. LESS PEOPLE.

GOOD LUCK, ZAN. TAKE CARE OF YOURSELF. AND GO EASY TODAY.
IT'S YOUR LAST BIT OF NORMAL FOR A WHILE.

Less than a week and I'll be at Base Camp.
Can't sleep. Can't breathe. Coughing all the time. One more day of acclimatizing.
The guidebooks say always climb higher. Get used to the lack of oxygen in the air, adjust the blood.

I have my own reasons.
Been seeing people who look out of place. My rusty alarms all screaming.

In the middle of nowhere, you recognize your own.
We're days away from a working phone. The mail takes forever.

The only strings tied to my old world left to burn are dead bodies.

Out here, that's easier than breathing.

MY PACK IS 70 POUNDS OR SO. AISHMA'S PACK IS ANOTHER 50. IT'S LIKE CARRYING MYSELF UP A HILL.
DORJE'S SUPPOSED TO CARRY IT. BE MY SUPPORT. BUT HE RAN.
I CAN'T BLAME HIM.
NO, I CAN. SCREW HIM.
NO ONE ELSE IS GOING TO DO THIS FOR YOU, ZAN.

HASKELL'S UP THERE. MARS IS UP THERE.
A SMALL ARMY. A HUGE JACKPOT.
YOU CAN DO THIS.
FUCK. YOU CAN'T DO THIS.

HEY.

DORJE! YOU ASSHOLE!
THANKS. NICE TO SEE YOU TOO.
SO, WHAT? NOW YOU'RE BACK IN?
NEVER LEFT, ZAN. I CAN'T LEAVE.
YOU'D DIE OUT THERE WITHOUT ME.

YET AGAIN: ASS. HOLE.
JUST ONCE, THOUGH, LET ME ASK YOU SOMETHING.
AND I WON'T EVER ASK AGAIN.
WHY ARE YOU DOING THIS?
BECAUSE IT'S THERE.

ISN'T THAT DANGEROUS, DORJE?
WHAT'S THAT?
SMOKING NEAR THE TANK OF COMPRESSED OXYGEN?

YOU HAVE YOUR OXYGEN. WE HAVE OURS.
LET'S MOVE OUT. WE'VE GOT A LONG WEEK AHEAD.

TONIGHT WE'LL REST IN TENGBOCHE. FROM THERE WE'LL PASS THROUGH PANGBOCHE, PHERICHE--
--THUKLA, LOBUCHE, GORAK SHEP, PHANTOM ALLEY, ALL THE WAY TO BASE CAMP.
I KNOW.
I'VE STUDIED THE MAPS. READ THE BOOKS. I'VE BEEN DREAMING ABOUT THIS FOR--

THERE SHE IS.
IS THAT...

ZAN?
YOU OKAY?
ZAN?

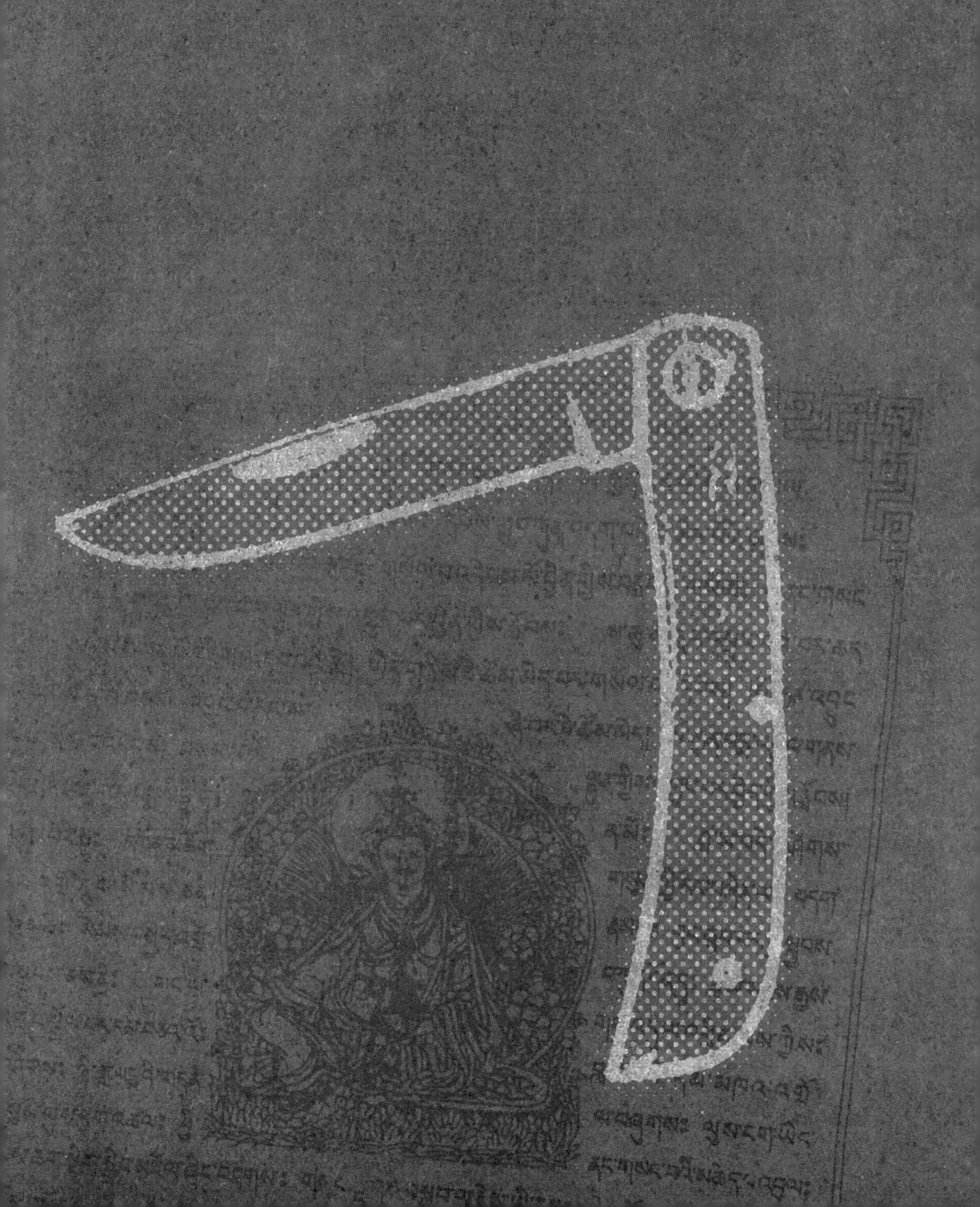

WHOLE NEW LEAF.

I USED TO TELL MYSELF THAT WHEN I FIXED MYSELF, I'D CLIMB TO THE ROOF OF THE WORLD.
BUT THEN I NEVER REALLY GOT AROUND TO GETTING CLEAN.

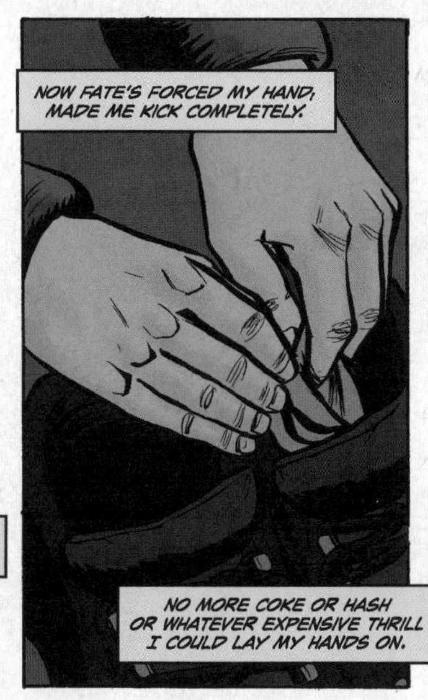
NOW FATE'S FORCED MY HAND, MADE ME KICK COMPLETELY.
NO MORE COKE OR HASH OR WHATEVER EXPENSIVE THRILL I COULD LAY MY HANDS ON.

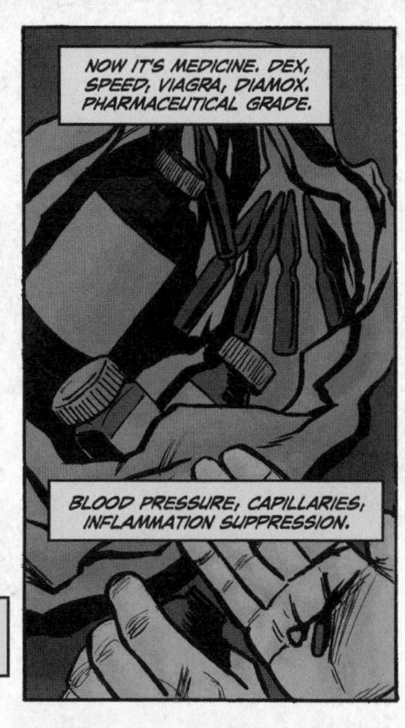
NOW IT'S MEDICINE. DEX, SPEED, VIAGRA, DIAMOX. PHARMACEUTICAL GRADE.
BLOOD PRESSURE; CAPILLARIES; INFLAMMATION SUPPRESSION.

IT ISN'T HABIT. IT'S SCIENCE.
PERFORMANCE ENHANCEMENT.

I LEFT ZAN JENSEN IN A DIRTY LODGE ROOM IN NAMCHE.
ALL HER PROBLEMS. ALL HER WORRIES. A CLEAN SLATE.
A NEW LEAF.
A BETTER LIFE. STARTING NOW.

"ZAN! WELCOME TO BASE CAMP."
"WHY'D YOU LET ME SLEEP SO LONG, DORJE?"
"YOU CAN'T CLIMB ON WILL ALONE. STILL NEED TO SLEEP. AND EAT."

SPEAKING OF, I GOT YOU A SANDWICH.
NOT HUNGRY.
YOU EAT, I'LL SHOW YOU THE SIGHTS. DEAL?

GIANT TENTS ARE PRO OUTFITS. HIMALAYAN DREAMS, ADVENTURE ASCENTS.
MY COUSIN WORKS FOR THEM. I GOT US A DINNER INVITATION.
MM. THOSE BIG TENTS ARE CHINESE, AMERICAN. THAT'S QATAR, I THINK?
I TOLD YOU, DORJE, I DON'T WANT TO SOCIALIZE.

"AND EVERYONE ELSE ARE NON-EXPEDITION CLIMBERS. I GOT IT."
"NOW *THEM*, THEY'RE THE TALK OF CAMP. SHERPAS SAY THEY KEEP TO THEMSELVES, HAVE A LOT OF MONEY BEHIND THEM.
"NO ONE HAS A CLUE WHO THEY ARE."
"I DO."

HUSTLE IT UP, PRICE.
IF I HAVE TO COME IN AND GET YOU, YOU'RE NEXT DOWN THE HOLE.
FUCK YOU, SONNY BOY.

OH, SORRY, MISS. I'LL COME B--
JESUS FUCKING CHRIST, HASKELL. YOUR-- YOUR **HAND**. I HOPED IT WAS-- THOUGHT--

SUZANNE?
WHAT IN THE HELL ARE YOU DOING HERE?

I HOPED IT WAS SOMEONE ELSE'S HAND I FOUND.
GOD, AFTER TENZING...
I TH-- I THOUGHT YOU WERE **DEAD**, HASKELL.
NOT YET.
YOU GOT YOUR ASS **AWAY** FROM THIS, SUZANNE. I TOLD MYSELF AT LEAST YOU GOT OUT OF THIS.
NOW **WHY** DID YOU **COME** HERE?
TO **RESCUE** YOU. TO KEEP THESE MURDERERS FROM GETTING AWAY WITH IT.
THEN WHY DIDN'T YOU JUST STAY PUT AND CALL THE POLICE?

YOU STOLE IT.
WHATEVER THEY WERE LOOKING FOR IN MARS'S STUFF.
AND WHAT'S UP **THERE**. YOU CAME TO STEAL IT OUT FROM UNDER THEM?
HOW CLOSE AM I?

I...
I CAN GET YOU OUT.
YOU--**WE** GO TO NAMCHE, FIND A DOCTOR, CALL SOMEONE.
GO HOME.
LEAVE IT ALONE, SUZANNE.
OUTSIDE THIS SHITHOUSE ARE SIX ARMED PSYCHOTICS WHO HAVEN'T KILLED ANYTHING IN DAYS.
ESPECIALLY YOU.
BECAUSE OF **ME**. I KEEP THEM MOVING, KEEP THEM FROM HURTING ANYONE ELSE.

HASKELL. STOP.
LISTEN. WE'LL FIGURE THIS OUT. JUST STAY HERE A SECOND.
CAN'T. I GAVE MY WORD.
I'M GETTING THESE FUCKERS TO THE TOP AND I'M GOING TO MAKE SURE WE NEVER COME DOWN. MARS INCLUDED.
I'M A DEAD MAN.
LET IT COUNT FOR SOMETHING.

EXCUSE ME?
CAN WE JOIN YOU?
THE CROWD IN HERE IS GIVING US A HEADACHE.
PLUS WE'RE DRIVING EACH OTHER NUTS.
SORRY IF WE'RE INTERRUPTING. YOU LOOKED LIKE OUR TYPE OF ANTISOCIAL.
YEAH, SURE. I'VE HARDLY TALKED TO ANYONE ALL DAY.

ALEX. HELL OF A SHINER YOU GOT.
LAURENN. FORGIVE OUR MANNERS.
FIVE WEEKS UP HERE AND WE'VE GONE FERAL.
HEY. I'M EMILY.

--SUDDENLY I WAS SELLING THE CAR AND BOOKING OUR SPOTS AND BAM, WE'RE ON A PLANE TO KATHMANDU.
LADY'S PERSUASIVE WHEN SHE WANTS TO BE.
SOUNDS EXCITING.
AND WHO'RE YOU CLIMBING WITH? I KNOW IT'S NOT US.
JUST ME. ME AND A SHERPA.

WOW. AIN'T *YOU* HARDCORE?
I TOLD HIM. *WE* SHOULD HAVE DONE IT LIKE THAT.
EH, KINDA GOT FORCED INTO IT BY A FRIEND.
SOUNDS LIKE A GOOD FRIEND.
IF YOU LIKE UNGRATEFUL ASSHOLES, SURE.

COMING TO THE PARTY? WE CAN STICK TOGETHER. LESS CHANCE OF ANYONE TALKING TO US.
PARTY? HERE?
SUMMIT ANNIVERSARY. A MILESTONE IN HUMANITY'S ONGOING "HEY, FUCK YOU" TO MOTHER NATURE.
WAIT HERE. I'LL GET THE PARTY FAVORS.

I ONLY GOT TWO CUPS, SO WE HAVE TO SHARE, BABE.
THAT'S OKAY. I'LL SKIP THE SPLITTING HANGOVER.
I'LL TAKE HER SHARE.
IS THAT MACALLAN?
GOOD EYE. BEEN CARRYING IT AROUND THE LAST TWO MONTHS.

SOME FOR NOW, THE REST UPON OUR TRIUMPHANT RETURN.
OKAY, ONE, BUT THEN WE HAVE TO GET TO SLEEP.
LIVE A BIT, LAURENN. WE COULD ALL BE DEAD IN A FEW DAYS.

HELL, IN A COUPLE HOURS.
SO YOU GET A BIT DARK WHEN YOU DRINK.

TRUST ME, NOT JUST WHEN I DR--

DIPSHIT! SLOW IT DOWN.
LET IT GO, ALEX.
NO WAY, SUZANNE, THERE'S NO EXCUSE FOR THAT.

...
I GOTTA GO.

DON'T. WE'RE SORRY. WE DIDN'T WANT TO--
WE'RE FANS.
GREAT. FORGET YOU SAW ME.
THANKS FOR THE DRINKS.

I HAD AN EX WHO ONCE TOLD ME; "YOU'RE PROGRAMMED TO ACCEPT THINGS."
THAT, AND AN OBNOXIOUS HABIT OF OCCASIONALLY BEING CORRECT, IS WHY THEY'RE AN EX.
ALL MY LIFE I ACCEPTED IT.

WHEN MY PARENTS SHIPPED ME FROM JERSEY TO NOWHERE, COLORADO. TO THE ACADEMY.
WHEN THEY HANDED ME MY COMPETITION SCHEDULE ON GRADUATION DAY.
WHEN MY FRIEND FIRST OFFERED ME A QUICK FIX IN A TURIN HOTEL SUITE.

AFTER I RAN, FOR A FEW MOMENTS, IT WAS MAGIC. A WORLD SPUN ON MY AXIS.
BECAUSE I LIVED IN A BUBBLE, EVERYTHING SEEMED INFINITE. UNTIL I STEPPED THROUGH IT.

THEN I SAW ALL THE UGLY BITS.
"REALLY? THIS IS IT?"

WHY SHOULD THIS BE ANY DIFFERENT?
THE SAME UGLY AMERICANS.
LYING TO DORJE.
HASKELL TELLING ME TO LEAVE.
SULLIVAN FUCKING MARS.

I CAN'T RUN ANYMORE.
I'VE BURNED ALL MY OTHER CHOICES.

AND I'M TRYING NOT TO GIVE IN.
TO FIGHT.
FIND A WAY OUT.

EVERYTHING IS FUCKED.
SO AM I.
BUT I'LL BE DAMNED IF I LIE DOWN AND TAKE IT ANYMORE.

THOSE WHO DO NOT REMEMBER THE PAST ARE CONDEMNED TO REPEAT IT.
Think of the worst thing you ever did.
Black days. Memories you wish you could redact.

If you're lucky, you only have a handful of those.
I have dozens.
Maybe hundreds.
Ambassador

All of them gladly forgotten in the frenzy of duty.
Too busy flying to the next op, undergoing my monthly evaluations.
Away from the Agency, they've begun rushing back in.

All the old ghosts coming back to haunt their owner.
MKE DIVISION
HUMAN ENGINEERING
Rebuilding my past one stone at a time.
HOME
PATRIOT
LOVE
Trying to make sense of nightmare logic.
GUN
ME
FATHER
FAMILY
MOTHER
SECRET
GOD
HERO
HAPPINESS
INNOCENT
KILL
ENEMY
Now think of the best thing you ever did.
How it obliterates everything bad that's come your way.
A car wash of the soul.
That's how Everest feels.
It feels like home.

PLANNING ON COMING OUT TODAY?
FUCK YOU. WHAT IF I WASN'T DECENT?
TOO EASY.
COME ON OUT.
CUTE MAP, DORJE.
IS THIS WHERE YOU EXPLAIN SHIT I ALREADY KNOW AGAIN?
SINCE YOU WON'T TELL ME WHAT YOU KNOW? YES.
I'M LEAVING FOR CAMP 1 IN A FEW. I'LL GET US SET UP.
I'LL BE OUT OF HERE BY 5 A.M.
BY FOUR. ONCE THE SUN COMES UP, THINGS GET TRICKY.
TALKED TO SOME CLIMBERS WHO LEFT THIS MORNING.
THEIR WEATHER WINDOW IS IN TWO DAYS.
I KNOW.
AND IN TWO DAYS, EVERYONE ON THE MOUNTAIN IS GOING TO BE SQUEEZING THROUGH IT.
SO WE JUST GET THERE AHEAD OF THE CROWD.
WE CAN DO THIS, DORJE.
IN ONE STRAIGHT PUSH.
WE CAN TRY.
BUT DON'T UNDERESTIMATE HOW EXHAUSTED WE'RE GOING TO BE.
THE ICEFALL. I KNOW. I'M READY.
MM. I'M NOT.
SORT OF.
NO MORE OF THESE FOR YOU.
AND NO MORE SWEARING, ZAN.

YOU PRUDE.
DON'T DISRESPECT HER, ZAN. BAD THINGS HAPPEN.
SHE'S NOT AS TOLERANT AS I AM WITH LYING, STEALING, AND FOUL MOUTHS.
WE'RE GOING TO NEED ALL THE HELP WE CAN GET.
AMEN.

THERE'S ABOUT THIRTY WAYS TO DIE ON EVEREST. FACTOR IN THE AGENTS AND IT DOUBLES.

IF I DIE UP THERE, I'LL BECOME ANOTHER BODY. ANOTHER SULLIVAN MARS.
SOME OTHER ENTERPRISING IDIOT'S POTENTIAL PAYDAY.
EXCEPT NO ONE WOULD PAY OUR PRICES TO BRING ME DOWN.

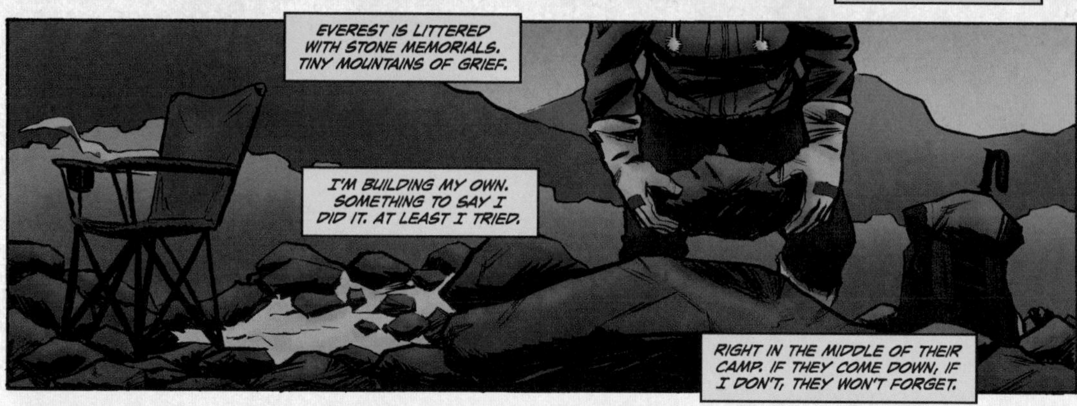
EVEREST IS LITTERED WITH STONE MEMORIALS. TINY MOUNTAINS OF GRIEF.
I'M BUILDING MY OWN. SOMETHING TO SAY I DID IT. AT LEAST I TRIED.
RIGHT IN THE MIDDLE OF THEIR CAMP. IF THEY COME DOWN, IF I DON'T, THEY WON'T FORGET.

I WANT THEM TO REMEMBER THE NAME OF THE ONE WHO FUCKED THEIR WORLD UP.
ZAN JENSEN

YOU'VE GOT THIS.
NO, YOU DON'T.

HELL, IT'S ONLY 3,000 FEET.
3,000 FEET OF SHIFTING GLACIER.

ONE FOOT IN FRONT OF THE OTHER.
YOU CAN STILL TURN AROUND. NO ONE WOULD BLAME YOU. NOT EVEN HASKELL.

OKAY. NICE AND SMOOTH.
OH GOD OH GOD OH GOD OH GOD OH GOD.

ARE YOU KIDDING ME?

PICK UP THE PACE, PRICE. I WANT TO GET IN A TENT.
WELL, Y'KNOW--
--MAYBE I'D MOVE A BIT FASTER IF YOU HADN'T CUT OFF MY *FUCKING HAND*.
BE GLAD WE LEFT YOU ONE, GRAVE ROBBER.
SO YOU GET UP THERE, DRAG MARS TO BASE CAMP, AND THEN WHAT?
WITH ANY LUCK, THEY GIVE US THE OKAY TO MACHINE-GUN EVERYONE ON THIS SHITTY ROCK.
AND ME?
WHAT *ABOUT* YOU?
I'M...
I'M... DONE.
I'VE SPENT MY LIFE LEADING AMATEURS PLACES THEY SHOULDN'T EVER BE.
I ALWAYS WANTED TO SAY THIS. YOU WANT UP THERE SO BAD? DO IT YOURSELF.
YOU'RE NOT GOING TO KILL ME, SONNY.
NOT AFRAID OF DYING?
CUTE.
THERE'S WORSE THINGS.
SMASHING YOUR TEETH OUT WITH A GUN, FOR ONE.
YOU WON'T DIE, BUT YOU'LL HAVE BIBLICAL LEVELS OF PAIN. EXPOSED-NERVE TRAUMA.
WHAT'S YOUR FEAR THRESHOLD THERE?

EASY AS PIE.
GRAAAHTT
FUCK.
REMEMBER THE LESSONS.
ON YOUR FEET, PRICE!
CONTROLLED BREATHING.
PRIME IT.
SAFETY OFF.
BREATHE.
THWUKK
THWUKK
HEH.
MISS JENSEN?
IS THAT YOU?
I HAVE TO SAY, YOU CERTAINLY ARE COMMITTED.
WE'LL KILL YOUR PARTNER, TAKE YOU APART, AND DROP YOU DOWN A DARK HOLE.
YOU AND YOUR SUBPAR AIM AREN'T GOING TO STOP US.
HASKELL, YOU WANNA TELL THEM WHY WE SHOULD BE AT CAMP I BY NOW?
HEH. HEH HEH. HA HA HA.
ONCE THE SUN COMES UP, THE ICEFALL MELTS.

SCATTER!
RUN, ZAN!
BRING THIS WHOLE GODDAMN ICEFALL DOWN ON OUR HEADS!
BLAM!
BLAM!
BLAM!
THWUKK
THWUKK
THWUKK

THWUKK
THWUKK
THWUKK
THWUKK
THWUKK
WE'VE GOT AMMUNITION AND TIME TO SPARE, MISS JENSEN.
WHY DON'T YOU COME OUT? MAYBE WE HAVE A JOB FOR YOU.
RUN, ZAN! GO!
NO MORE RUNNING.
BLAM!
BLAM!
BLAM!
THWUKK
THWUKK
THWUKK
FWOOOMP

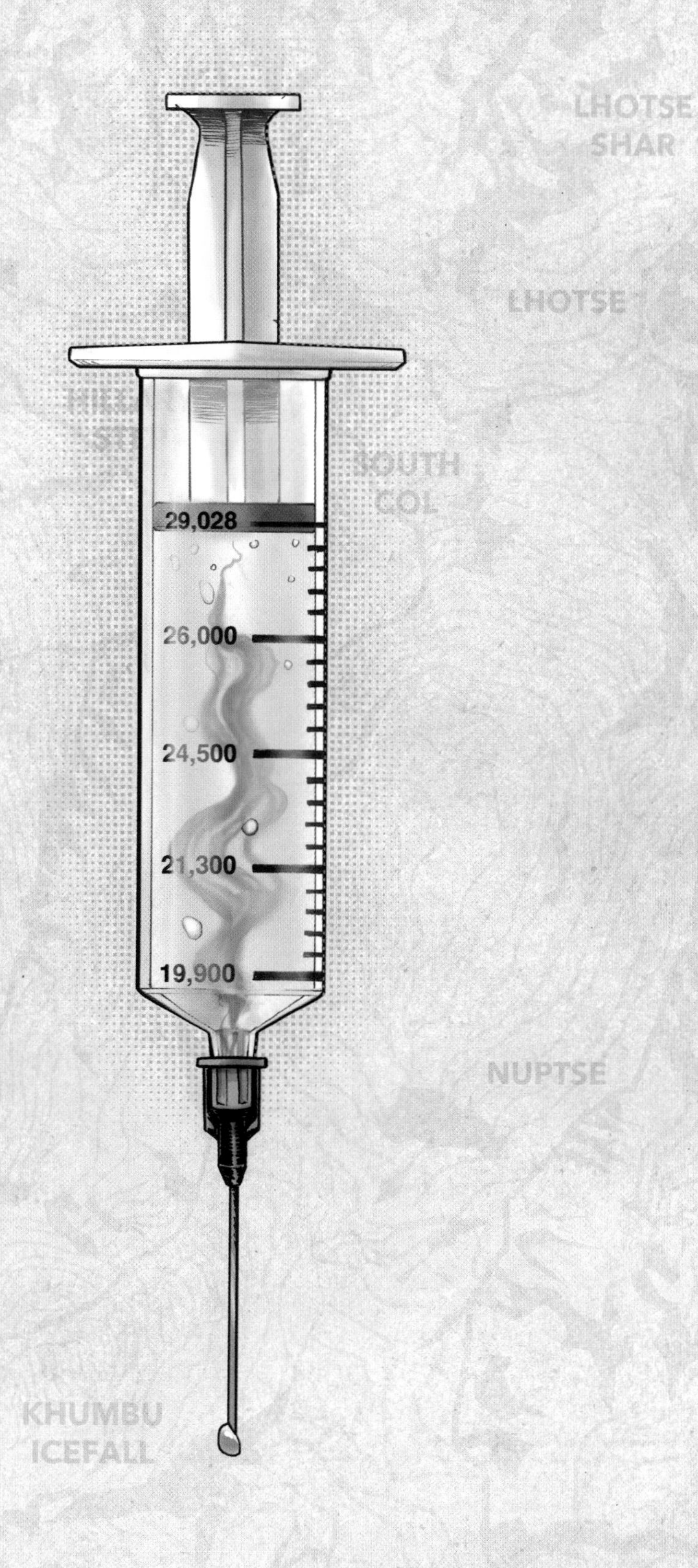

LHOTSE
SHAR
LHOTSE
SOUTH
COL
29,028
26,000
24,500
21,300
19,900
NUPTSE
KHUMBU
ICEFALL
BASE CAMP

ssport, NRN Card लगायत वितरण गर्ने
य दिइ[illegible] [illegible] बजे सम्म तोकिएकोले
ह व्यह[illegible] सवारी[illegible] था सम्वन्धित सबैलाई
कारीक[illegible] गर्न [illegible]न्छ ।

YOU SPEND ENOUGH TIME ON A MOUNTAIN, PEOPLE WILL TALK YOUR EAR OFF ABOUT AVALANCHES.

THE BIG, BAD NIGHTMARES OF WINTER SPORTS.

HOW TO WATCH FOR THEM.

HOW TO GET OUT OF THEIR WAY.

HOW TO SURVIVE IF YOU GET HIT.

IT'S LIKE FLIGHT ATTENDANTS EXPLAINING EMERGENCY LANDING PROCEDURE.

THE FIRST TIME, YOU LISTEN. THE FIFTH TIME YOU SKIM. EVENTUALLY YOU TUNE IT OUT.

AND EVERY TIME, YOU THINK TO YOURSELF, "NOT ME."

"NOT IT."

THIS WOULD BE A GOLD-MEDAL PERFORMANCE.

BUT IF THERE WAS A CATEGORY FOR STUPIDEST SHIT I'VE EVER DONE...

MY LIFE AS A SCORECARD. MAKES SENSE.

THEY'LL SAY I SHOWED PROMISE. THAT I FELL VICTIM TO FAME AND MONEY AND LIFE. THEY'LL ADD ME UP.

"HER SKYROCKETING CAREER...HER FALL FROM GRACE...HER SHAMEFUL RUN FROM JUSTICE..."

IN MY MEMORIAL THEY'LL MENTION "HER LOVING FAMILY."

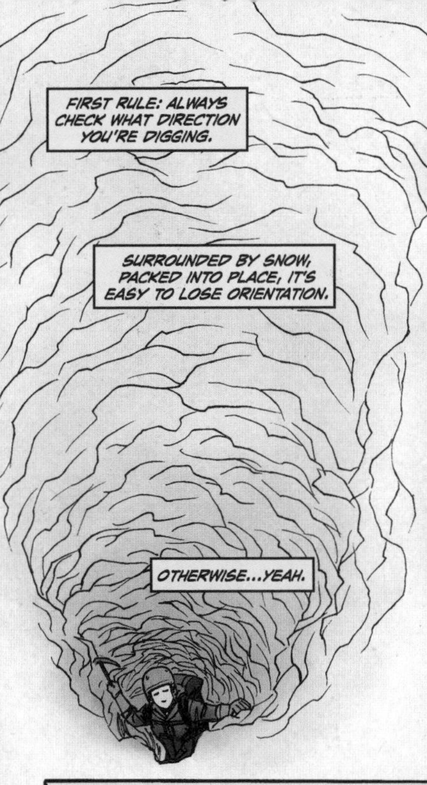
FIRST RULE: ALWAYS CHECK WHAT DIRECTION YOU'RE DIGGING.
SURROUNDED BY SNOW, PACKED INTO PLACE, IT'S EASY TO LOSE ORIENTATION.
OTHERWISE...YEAH.

SECOND RULE: DITCH YOUR PACK, ANYTHING THAT'S WEIGHING YOU DOWN.
I'VE DONE TOO MUCH OF THAT.

SURE, IT'S FULL OF THINGS THAT COULD SAVE MY LIFE.
BUT ALL I CAN THINK OF ARE THE MEDALS.

CAN FEEL THEM THROUGH THE BOTTOM OF THE BAG.
I WORKED TOO HARD TO EARN THEM, FOUGHT TOO HARD TO KEEP THEM.
TOO HARD TO LEAVE THEM TO VANISH IN A GLACIER.
TOO HARD TO SAVE MYSELF INSTEAD OF THEM.

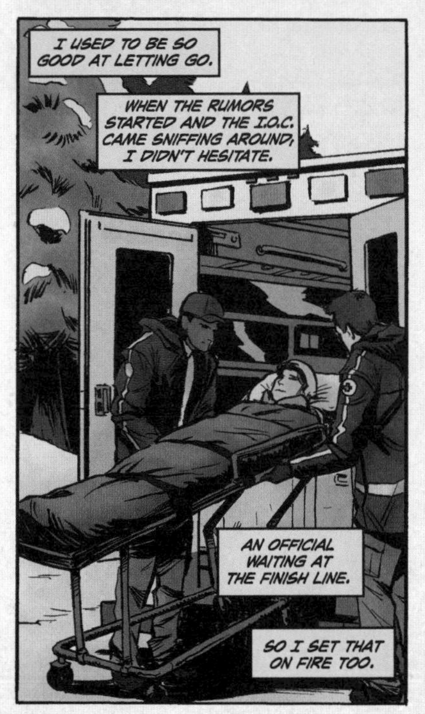
I USED TO BE SO GOOD AT LETTING GO.
WHEN THE RUMORS STARTED AND THE I.O.C. CAME SNIFFING AROUND, I DIDN'T HESITATE.
AN OFFICIAL WAITING AT THE FINISH LINE.
SO I SET THAT ON FIRE TOO.

DAD LOVED TO TALK SHOP AT DINNER. STORIES OF D.U.I. DRUNKS IN HIS AMBULANCE, FAKING INJURIES TO ESCAPE A BREATHALYZER.
"THE KEY IS TO COMMIT, NO MATTER HOW DUMB OR DOOMED IT SEEMS," HE ONCE SAID.
"LIFE LESSONS," HE'D TELL MY HORRIFIED MOM.

I CAN'T REMEMBER WHAT HE SOUNDS LIKE, BUT I REMEMBER THAT.
IT'S SO WARM IN HERE. HOT EVEN.
SHOULD REST.
TAKE A BREAK.
TAKE...
TAKE IT...
TAKE...

TAKE IT, ZAN! TAKE MY HAND!
I'VE GOT YOU.
AM I DEAD?
SORRY TO INFORM YOU, BUT NO.
YOU'RE STILL WITH US.

COME ON. LET IT GO. WE'LL COME BACK FOR IT.
NO! I NEED IT. FOR THE CLIMB.
CLIMB'S OVER, ZAN. PEOPLE COULD BE DEAD DOWN THERE.
JUST GET ME TO THE TENT.
LET ME SLEEP.
LITTLE BIT FURTHER. FIRST AID, HOT TEA, AND BAD FOOD AWAIT.
THEN WE'LL START FIGURING OUT HOW TO GET DOWN.

WHO'S "WE," DORJE?
ZAN, YOU CAN'T--
I'M NOT CLOSE TO DONE.
I'M GETTING TO THE SUMMIT.
WITH OR WITHOUT YOU.
WHEN I SAID TO LET IT GO, ZAN?
I DIDN'T MEAN THE PACK.

GODDAMN--
SAVE YOUR VOICE, ZAN. BREATHE. AND PLEASE STOP SWEARING.
WE'RE STUCK FOR THE NIGHT. WAITING FOR A TEAM FROM BASE CAMP TO COME CLEAR A PATH.
I DON'T *NEED* OXYGEN.
YOU'VE BEEN ASLEEP FOR A DAY. YOU'RE A WALKING BRUISE. YOU NEED TO HEAL.
WE'RE WASTING IT. I'M GONNA SHUT THIS OFF.
FINE. STOP. I'LL DO IT. DO YOU SEE HOW OUT OF IT YOU ARE?
LOOK AT YOUR HANDS.
A SPECK OF THIS LIP BALM ALL OVER THEM MEETS THE VALVE? YOU TRYING TO BLOW US ALL UP?
TOO LATE. ALREADY DID THAT.

TAKE SMALL SIPS. THEN IT'S BACK ON OXYGEN, BACK TO SLEEP FOR YOU.
WE CAN TALK LATER.
NOTHING TO TALK ABOUT. UNLESS YOU WANT TO GIVE ME ONE OF THOSE SMOKES?

DID THEY FIND ANYONE ELSE DOWN IN THE ICEFALL?
I DON'T KNOW, ZAN. I'VE BEEN BUSY KEEPING YOU ALIVE.
MOST LIKELY NO ONE ALIVE.

STAY. BREATHE. ENJOY THE MIRACLE OF NOT DYING OR BEING SERIOUSLY INJURED.
LOVE YOU TOO, PARTNER.

YOU'RE HIGH ON OXYGEN.
AMONG OTHER THINGS.

HALO THANGBU.
NYEP CHIK?
THANGBU WONGGUP. LAS.

HOW MANY THEY DIG OUT?
FIVE, MAYBE. THEY SAY THAT'S ALL OF THEM, BUT SHERPA SAY TWO MISSING FROM GROUP.
WE'RE FINE. THANK YOU FOR YOUR CONCERN, BUT WE'RE FINE. JUST GO.
WE'LL BE OUT OF YOUR HAIR IN A DAY OR TWO.
WHY WOULD THEY LIE?

HEY, I KNOW YOU, RIGHT? YOU'RE A GUIDE, YEAH?
USED TO BE. A LONG TIME AGO.

THESE DAYS I'M EVEN WORSE.

HA. YES. SEEMS TO BE GOING AROUND.

"GOOD LUCK. STAY SAFE."

Climbing a mountain is like killing someone.
The trick is to focus on yourself.

There's so many details you can get lost in.
The smell of gunpowder and blood.
The sharp battery taste of adrenaline in your mouth.
The crunch of snow like white noise.
The look on their faces through a scope or a keyhole or a car window.
That second before they realize that everything is moving too fast to stop.

You have to focus: on your breathing, every muscle's movement, one step to the next, regimented.
The mountain, the man at the end of your knife: they're your enemies.
You can't give in. Not to wonder nor sympathy nor fear.

It's not that the fear isn't there.
You just have to be louder.
It's Them vs. Us.

Always has been.

Thought I'd thrown their trail back in Namche, but they keep coming back, my little Agency babies.
I see their eyes glance over to the back of my hand, my thigh, to where I've got the microfilm stashed.
Asking where I'm from in that knowing way.
I smell blood on them.
Or maybe that's me.
This makes four since I got to Base Camp.
They try blending in, ghosting as climbers. But I can tell.
I find them.
I deal with them.
No feelings, no thoughts.
It's a job. Like climbing.
You can walk away from a job, but that doesn't mean it won't come with you when you go.
And that you won't be grateful for it.
You set a goal and march towards it, over anyone and anything in your way.
Daddy tanned my hide for thinking like that.
My country gave me awards for it.

AS A GUIDE, I UNDERSTAND ENOUGH OF THE SHERPA LANGUAGE TO KNOW CERTAIN USEFUL WORDS AND PHRASES.
SURVIVOR, FOR ONE.

FIVE, FOR ANOTHER.
ALL I CAN THINK OF IS THE GUN I LOST IN THE ICEFALL.

IT HAD AT LEAST FIVE BULLETS IN IT.

TAKING ADVICE FROM A DEAD MAN. TRYING TO AVENGE ANOTHER DEAD MAN.
WHAT THE HELL IS WRONG WITH ME?

KAFF K-KAFF
CHRIST ON A BIKE.

HE'S STILL ALIVE.
THERE'S A CHANCE.

I ALWAYS WANTED TO SAVE THE DAY.

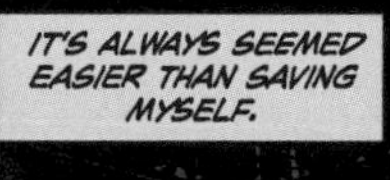
IT'S ALWAYS SEEMED EASIER THAN SAVING MYSELF.

BACK UP!
ZAN! IT'S DORJE.
CALM DOWN.

SORRY. BAD DREAMS.
YES. THAT ABOUT SUMS THINGS UP.

LET'S PACK UP. THE ICEFALL IS CLEAR.
IF WE'RE NOT THROUGH BY NOON, IT MIGHT AVALANCHE AGAIN.

NO.
SHE'S NOT WORTH DYING FOR.

YES, SHE IS. WHEN YOU DON'T HAVE ANYTHING ELSE, SHE'S WORTH IT.
SO I'M NOT WALKING AWAY, NOT AFTER I'VE COME THIS FAR.

YOU CAN'T DO THIS, ZAN.
YOU'RE NOT ABLE. NOT IN THE STATE YOU'RE IN.
I AM. YOU JUST HAVE TO HELP ME.

YOU NEED TO INJECT ME.
NO, ZAN. I'M NOT DOING ANY OF THIS. HELPING YOU DIE HERE.
YOU *GOT* TO CAMP IV, DORJE. YOU AT LEAST *SAW* THE TOP.
GIVE ME THAT CHANCE.
I CAN MAKE THE CLIMB. I JUST NEED SOMETHING TO GET ME BY. DISTRACT ME FROM THE PAIN.

YOU'RE LOOKING OUT FOR ME. I GET THAT.
FACE IT, YOU CAN'T FUCK ME UP ANY MORE THAN I ALREADY AM.

HELP ME TO CAMP II. YOU STILL WANT TO GO AFTER THAT, YOU CAN.
C'MON, YOU OWE ME THAT.

THIS ISN'T SMART, ZAN. THE SEASON IS WRONG.
WANTING IT ISN'T ENOUGH. YOU HAVE TO FIGHT, TOOTH AND NAIL.
YOU HAVE TO RESPECT HER.

CHOMOLUNGMA ISN'T A *THING* TO BE CONQUERED. SHE'S A GODDESS. SHE'S UNPREDICTABLE. AND NOW SHE'S ANGRY.
NOT AS ANGRY AS ME.

THIRTY MINUTES. WE STILL HAVE TO PACK YOUR TENT.
I ONLY NEED TEN.
FEELING BETTER THEN?

THE HARDEST LIE IS YOUR FIRST. DECIDING THAT YOU'RE GOING TO POISON THIS NEW PATCH OF EARTH WITH A LANDMINE YOU ALWAYS HAVE TO REMEMBER IS THERE.
YES, DORJE. THANK YOU. YOU'RE A LIFESAVER.

AFTER THAT, THE REST ARE ALMOST EAGER TO LINE UP, THEY'RE SO DAMN EASY.

WAKING UP AFTER THE ICEFALL, MY WHOLE BODY WAS A BRUISE.
NOTHING SOME ASPIRIN AND OXYGEN DIDN'T TAKE CARE OF.
I DIDN'T NEED THE INJECTION.
IT'S ALL I COULD COME UP WITH.
PHYSICAL BLACKMAIL.
FAKE AN INJURY, GARNER SYMPATHY. GET OUT OF JAIL.

I KNEW IF I COULD GET HIM TO DO IT, I COULD GET HIM TO KEEP GOING WITH ME.
TO NOT LEAVE ME ALONE.
THAT LOOK ON HIS FACE AFTER THE NEEDLE SANK HOME--WE BOTH KNEW HE DIDN'T HAVE A CHOICE.

THAT'S A LIE I'M USED TO TELLING.

I'D FEEL BAD, EXCEPT I FEEL SO GOOD.
ONE SOLID PUSH OF MY TOES AGAINST THE EARTH AND I'D DRIFT UP TO THE SUMMIT.
DORJE QUIETLY, ANGRILY DRAGGED UP AFTER ME.
IT'S FINE. POETIC, EVEN.
WE'RE IN THE HEART OF THE WESTERN CWM, CUT OFF FROM THE WINDS. YOU CAN HEAR A CLIMBER SNEEZE A MILE AWAY.
THE VALLEY OF SILENCE.
PLEASE SLOW DOWN, DORJE.
THE CWM IS AN ICE-COVERED BOWL. THE SUN'S SOLAR RADIATION DUMPS DOWN ON US, ROLLING AROUND.
IT'S LIKE HIKING THROUGH A RUNNING MICROWAVE.
IF YOU TALK TOO MUCH, YOU CAN SUNBURN THE ROOF OF YOUR MOUTH.
FORGET TO WEAR YOUR GOGGLES AND YOU CAN FRY YOUR CORNEAS. BLIND AT 20,000 FEET.
AND THIS IS THE EASIEST PART OF THE CLIMB.
THE SILENCE IS NICE.
WHAT WOULD I SAY ANYWAY?
"I'M SORRY"?

HATE TO BREAK IT TO YOU.

WE'VE GOT A TRAFFIC JAM AHEAD OF US.

"ZAN, PLEASE. PAY ATTENTION."

YEAH. SORRY. IT'S... THAT.
"WHAT'S THE PROBLEM?
"YOU NEVER SAW A BODY BEFORE?"

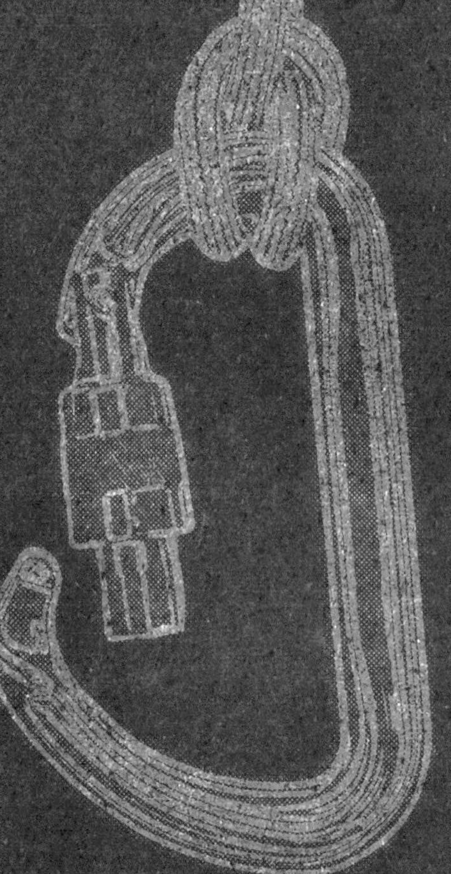

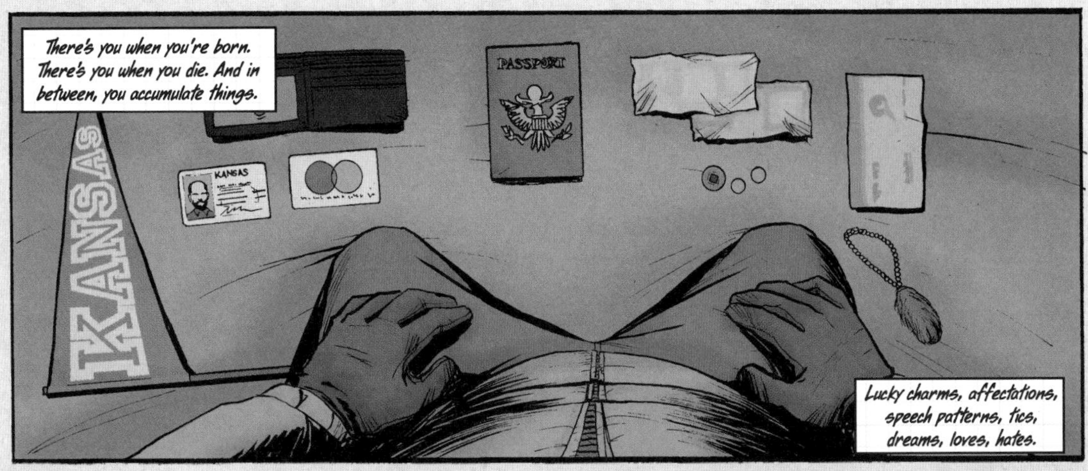
There's you when you're born. There's you when you die. And in between, you accumulate things.
PASSPORT
KANSAS
KANSAS
Lucky charms, affectations, speech patterns, tics, dreams, loves, hates.

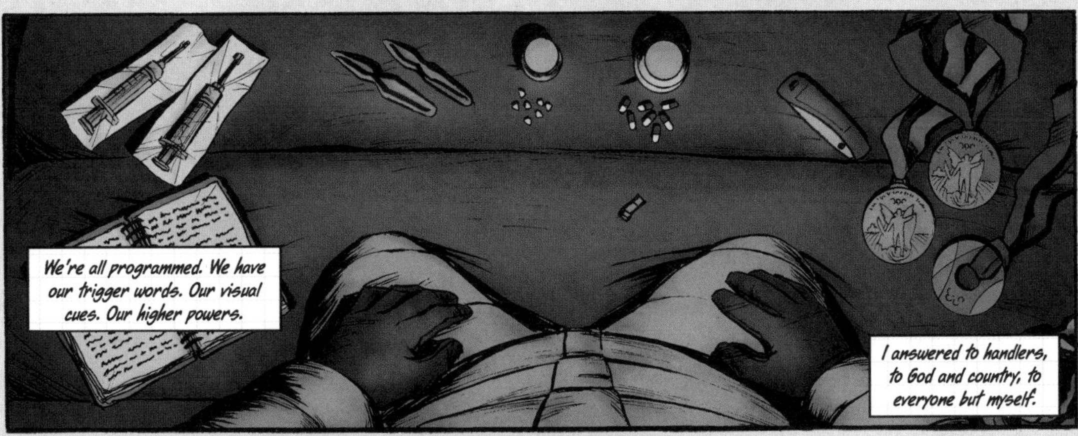
We're all programmed. We have our trigger words. Our visual cues. Our higher powers.
I answered to handlers, to God and country, to everyone but myself.

I was fortunate. I didn't have to. Life makes sense when someone is holding your hand.
And when they're gone, you reach out for something else.
Only up here there's no one to take your hand. No one cares about you.
Every man for himself.
Everyone too busy trying to stay alive to see beyond themselves.
Selfishness is useful. No one notices me, my Agency shadows, or their bodies I leave behind me as I go.
No one pays attention to the bodies.
Who would be dumb enough to care?

ZAN? YOU AWAKE?
FOOD'S READY.
I DID WHAT I SAID I WOULD, WHAT MY CONSCIENCE REQUIRES OF ME. I GOT YOU THIS FAR.
SO NOW I HAVE TO FIGURE OUT WHAT TO DO NEXT. AND WHY WE'RE DOING IT.

WHO EXACTLY IT IS I'M REALLY CLIMBING WITH.

YOU'RE NOT SOME EVEREST NUT. THAT'S NOT WHAT'S DRIVING YOU. THAT'S NOT WHY YOU'RE HERE.
THAT'S NOT WHY YOU SEEM TO WANT TO DIE.

I'M SORRY TO PRY, BUT IT'S NOT AS IF YOU'RE GOING TO TELL ME WHAT I WANT TO KNOW.

"EVEN IF YOU WERE AWAKE."

Everything changes at some point.
After years of sudden shifts in direction, you can almost smell the turns coming on.
You assume crash position, fold up, and wait for impact.
They can teach you everything except what to do when the crash doesn't come.
When the ship keeps going, when the bodies don't fall.
When it's only yourself to blame.
So you stay where you know or run where you don't.
Halfway to the top now, my thoughts are getting clearer as the air gets thinner.
I can see everything laid out behind me like I never could before. Memories, missions, immaterial moments that haunt me.
Tiny little cracks in what I thought I knew.
Maybe it's because I'm sick now. Coughing enough to break a rib.
Headaches that last for hours. No appetite. Can't take my boots off for fear of what I'd find.
I feel dead. Dying.
And I wonder if maybe that's why I came here in the first place.
For the man who lived quietly, tucked away from entanglements like friends and family--
--Everest makes a hell of a headstone.

I LOVE DRUGS.
I LOVE EVERYTHING ABOUT THEM.
IT'S THE RITUAL. I'M A SLAVE TO RITUAL.
PILLS RATTLING AGAINST EACH OTHER, BREAKING A CHUNK OFF A BRICK, PIPES AND RUBBER TUBING AND PLASTIC BAGGIES. FOLDED PAPER WITH TIGERS STAMPED ON THEM.
THE TRANSITION FROM THE RITUAL OF SPORTS TO THE RITUAL OF DRUGS IS PRETTY SIMPLE.
LOTS OF METHODICAL PREPARATION, ALL FOR A FEW MINUTES OF RUSHING JOY.
THEN YOU'RE BACK TO BEING HUMAN AND YOU JUST WANT IT AGAIN AND AGAIN AND AGAIN.
I LINE THEM UP EVERY MORNING AND SWALLOW THEM DOWN. CAPSULED COURAGE.
VIAGRA DILATES THE BLOOD VESSELS ENOUGH TO KEEP FLUID OUT OF MY LUNGS.
ASPIRIN FOR MY HEART, LOW-GRADE ACHES AND PAINS.
DEX TO KEEP MY BRAIN FROM SWELLING.
AMPHETAMINES TO KEEP ME MOVING.
MORPHINE TO KEEP ME HIGH.
BEING FUCKED UP SEEMS LIKE THE ONLY MOVE I CAN COUNT ON ANYMORE.
ANOTHER COCKTAIL TO KEEP THE FEAR AWAY.

BUT NOT THE NIGHTMARES.
BL-DEEP
BL-DEEP
BL-DEEP

NOT ENOUGH DRUGS IN THE WORLD TO MAKE THOSE GO AWAY.
BL-DEEP
BL-DEEP

I ALWAYS KNEW THE CRASH WAS COMING.
I'D DODGED BLOOD TESTS AND URINE SAMPLES. I HAD A GREAT LAWYER AND A PHOTOGENIC SMILE TO HIDE BEHIND.
I TOLD EVERYONE I WAS FINE.
HIDING YOUR REAL SELF FROM THE PEOPLE YOU LOVE IS EASY. THEY LET YOU.
WHICH MAKES THE REST OF THE WORLD YOUR ENEMY.
YOU'RE ALWAYS WAITING TO BE FOUND OUT. YOU DARE THEM TO.
AND YOU DRAG ANYONE UNLUCKY ENOUGH TO BE NEAR YOU DOWN WITH.
I ALWAYS WANTED THE ABILITY TO VANISH; TO DISAPPEAR INSIDE MYSELF. I WANTED TO BE NORMAL.
IGNORED BY THE EYES OF THE WORLD, INSTEAD OF TRACKED BY THEM.
TO HAVE MY SHITTY LITTLE LIFE LEFT UNEXAMINED; THE WAY DEAD ENDS SHOULD BE.
WHAT THEY WANTED TO FIND IN MY SYSTEM, THEY NEVER WOULD. I WASN'T DOPING. IT WASN'T ABOUT MAKING MYSELF BETTER.
IT WAS ABOUT NEVER HAVING TO CHANGE; TO KEEP LIVING A LIFE I HATED.
I LEFT WITH MY GYM BAG AND AN IDEA.
I DIDN'T TELL HER WHAT I WAS GOING TO DO. I DIDN'T WANT HER TO CONVINCE ME THERE WAS ANOTHER WAY.
I'D RIDDEN THE COURSE A DOZEN TIMES. I KNEW THE PERFECT SPOT.
I DIDN'T LOOK BACK. I WAS AFRAID TO.
THEY NEVER GAVE ME A CHANCE.
IT'S NOT MY FAULT PEOPLE GET HURT.
I'M TOO SHATTERED TO BE RESPONSIBLE.

HELLO, SUZANNE. CAN WE TALK?
WE'VE TALKED ONCE BEFORE. BACK IN KATHMANDU. ON THE PHONE? YOU REMEMBER?
AH. WELL, I'M NOT OFFENDED. YOU'VE HAD A LOT ON YOUR MIND. LIKE KILLING MY MEN.
WHAT DO YOU WANT? I'LL SCREAM BEFORE YOU CAN MAKE A MOVE ON ME.
AND THEN I'LL SHOVE THE KNIFE IN MY POCKET IN YOUR FACE, JUST TO BE SAFE.

CHARMING. WE'RE NOT GOING TO DO ANYTHING. WE JUST WANTED YOU TO KNOW WE KNOW YOU'RE HERE.
BUT TELL ME-- MY OWN CURIOSITY. WHAT HAPPENED TO ZAN JENSEN, AMERICA'S SWEETHEART?
DON'T KNOW HER. I KNOW THE ZAN WHO SHREDDED YOUR BUDDY'S FACE WITH HER CRAMPONS.

I KNOW THE ZAN WHO SENT A FUCKING MOUNTAIN DOWN ON YOUR HEADS.
THE ONE WHO'S GOING TO BEAT YOU TO MARS.

THAT'S THE ONLY ZAN AROUND ANY...
GOOD. THE GANG'S ALL HERE. EXCEPT FOR ONE. HE'S WATCHING HASKELL.
WE'D CONSIDERED KNEECAPPING HIM, BUT, YOU KNOW, THE SCREAMING AND ALL.
LET'S TALK.

YOU CAN PUT THE KNIFE AWAY, SUZANNE.
IF WE'D WANTED YOU DEAD, WE'D HAVE THROWN YOUR TENT INTO THE CREVASSE LAST NIGHT.
I DON'T KNOW WHAT THIS IS, THEN.
THIS IS A NEGOTIATION, SUZANNE.
OR A WARNING. YOU CAN CALL IT WHAT YOU LIKE.
GREAT. LET HASKELL GO AND THEN LEAVE.
IF YOU WANT MARS'S BODY, PAY US AND WE'LL GO GET IT.
HA HA HA.
NO. SUZANNE, YOU'VE GOT THIS ALL WRONG. I'M NOT AUTHORIZED TO NEGOTIATE.
HE IS.
HELLO?
SUZANNE JENSEN. DO I HAVE TO READ OFF ALL YOUR STATS OR CAN WE SKIP TO THE MEN IN FRONT OF YOU WITH GUNS AND NOTHING RESEMBLING MORAL JUDGMENT?
GOOD. I'M ONLY GOING TO SAY ALL THIS ONCE, SO PLEASE FOCUS. IT'S GOING TO MAKE WHAT HAPPENS NEXT A SWEET RELEASE OR THE WORST THING TO EVER HAPPEN TO YOU.

YOU ARE IN THE MIDST OF WHAT CAN BEST BE TERMED A CLUSTERFUCK.
YOU'VE MURDERED FEDERAL AGENTS. YOU'RE WANTED FOR A HOST OF OTHER CHARGES TOO MINOR TO MENTION.

SO THIS IS WHERE YOU STAND DOWN, ZAN.
PACK YOUR TRASH. WE'LL LET YOU GO. YOU HAVE FIVE MINUTES.

I DON'T THINK FEDERAL AGENTS MURDERING A MEMBER OF THE KATHMANDU POLICE OR TORTURING AN AMERICAN CITIZEN IS EXACTLY--
NO ONE CARES WHAT YOU THINK, JENSEN. YOU'RE A DOCUMENTED FUCKUP, DOING WHAT YOU DO, WHICH IS TO FUCK THINGS UP.
WE'RE THE GOVERNMENT.
WE'VE MADE LOUDER NOISES THAN YOU AND YOUR PARTNER DISAPPEAR.

THEN DO IT. SEE HOW EASILY I DISAPPEAR. YOUR MEN? THEY'RE ROOKIES UP HERE. THEY'RE GOING TO DIE AT THE FIRST BIT OF TECHNICAL CLIMBING WITHOUT US.
YOU NEED HASKELL ALIVE, SO YOU NEED ME ALIVE.
DO YOU THINK HE'D GIVE HIS LIFE FOR YOU?

HE ALREADY GAVE UP A HAND. WHAT DO YOU THINK?

HOW ABOUT YOUR OTHER PARTNER? THE SHERPA? DORJE? HE HAS A FAMILY THAT RELIES ON HIM. DID YOU KNOW THAT?

YOU DON'T GET IT. YOU CAN'T THREATEN ME. I DON'T CARE ANYMORE.
THEN WE'RE DONE. HAND THE PHONE BACK TO MY AGENT.
YOU NOW HAVE THREE MINUTES TO LET HIM KNOW YOUR DECISION.
NO, I'LL TELL YOU RIGHT NOW. GO FUCK YOURSELF.
COME AND GET ME YOURSELF. YOU KNOW WHERE I AM.

HI, ALEX.
ZAN!
GUYS, PLEASE. CAN WE NOT?
SORRY. IT'S EMILY. RIGHT.
WE'RE JUST-- WE FELT LIKE IDIOTS AFTER WE SHOT OFF OUR MOUTHS DOWN AT...
WAIT, HOW THE HELL DID YOU GET UP HERE SO FAST?
TOLD YOU WE SHOULD TEAM UP WITH HER.
GIRL'S GONNA SUMMIT BEFORE WE EVEN GET TO CAMP III.
C'MON, EMILY. YOUR FOOD'S ON US, OKAY?
IT'S THE LEAST WE CAN DO, RIGHT?
RIGHT.
LISTEN, WE HAVEN'T TOLD ANYONE. WE CAN RESPECT YOUR PRIVACY AND ALL THAT.
AND FOR WHATEVER IT'S WORTH? I NEVER BELIEVED ALL THOSE CHARGES AGAINST YOU.
YOU SHOULD HAVE.
I'M GUILTY AS SHIT.

OUR EXPEDITION LEADER HAS BEEN HOLDING HIS BREATH, WATCHING THE WEATHER. IF THINGS GET WORSE, HE'LL TURN US AROUND.

THIS IS WHAT WE GET. PLAYING IT SAFE. PUT ALL THE POWER IN THEIR HANDS. IT'S NOT THEIR DREAM, NOT THEIR MONEY. THEY DON'T HAVE TO--

NOT SURE WHY I TOLD YOU ALL THAT.
DO YOU STILL HAVE THAT BOTTLE, ALEX?
KAFF KAFF
IF I HADN'T LEFT IT AT BASE CAMP, YOU'D HAVE TO RACE ME TO THE BOTTOM.

I'M NOT CRAZY, YOU KNOW.
I'M NOT A LIAR EITHER. OR WHATEVER ELSE THEY'VE SAID ABOUT ME.
WE DIDN'T SAY YOU WERE.

I DON'T THINK I'D BELIEVE ME.
WHY-- *KAFF* WHY TELL US?
I DON'T KNOW. I WISH I KNEW WHY. WHY I'M DOING ANY OF THIS.

NOW YOU KNOW MORE ABOUT ME THAN ANYONE IN THE WORLD.
EVEN THESE ASSHOLES.
STAY AWAY FROM THEM.
AND ME.

I TRIED REHAB ONCE. QUIETLY.
I DIDN'T GET MUCH OUT OF IT BEFORE QUIETLY CHECKING MYSELF OUT. I DIDN'T WANT TO GET MUCH OUT OF IT. BUT I REMEMBERED THIS ONE BIT.

CONFESSION'S GOOD FOR THE SOUL.
IT'S BEEN SO LONG SINCE I LEVELED WITH ANYONE. THEY WERE RIGHT ABOUT THAT PART.

MAYBE THEY WERE RIGHT ABOUT THE OTHER STUFF.
WISH I STILL HAD A CHANCE TO FIND OUT.

One of the perks of Agency life was a short memory.
You filed each mission away to make room for the next.
You were grateful to be free. They were closed chapters.
But the further away I get, they're all opening back up.
I don't remember fear or joy or even that strung-out postadrenaline high I get every day up here.
It's all pictures, like a flipbook of moments.
In them, I'm moving without thinking.
Without knowing or caring what will happen next.
Just trusting it will work out. It always has before.

Except there are all these memories that don't make sense.
Parts that feel like someone pasted a fake page over the real one, a series of possible outcomes.

But I remember each one, like something watched more than lived, and each one seems real enough.
A series of glitches. Things that shouldn't be in there.
All of them accompanied by something like guilt.

Or what I remember guilt feeling like. It's been so long.
I have to remind myself where I am. What it does to the body, to the mind. But if memories are that easily misled, what about the rest of me?

How many betrayals will I have to go through?

Deep down I have a terrifying thought.
I'm starting to wonder if I belong on Everest.

Is this a glitch too?

THE AGENTS STOLE MY FOOD. MY BOTTLE OF OXYGEN. MY DRUGS.
WHAT THEY DIDN'T STEAL, THEY DESTROYED.
I CAN'T FIND THE MICROFILM. MY INSURANCE POLICY; THE ONE LITTLE BIT OF POWER I HAD; IS GONE.
THEY WANT TO CHASE ME OFF THE MOUNTAIN. THEY THINK IT'S THAT EASY.
BUT I HAVE EVERYTHING I NEED ON ME. MY MEDALS. MARS'S JOURNAL. A REASON TO GET TO THE SUMMIT.
I KNOW WHERE TO GET THE REST.

DORJE? I KNOW YOU'RE MAD AT ME, BUT I NEED YOUR HELP.
OKAY, COMING IN.

DORJE, COME ON, WAKE UP.
GO AWAY, ZAN.
I DON'T THINK YOU'RE HEARING ME. I NEED--

THIS IS NOT ABOUT WHAT YOU NEED.
I'M HERE TO CLIMB MY MOUNTAIN.
NOT TO HELP YOU DO WHATEVER YOU'RE DOING.

AT LEAST NO MORE THAN YOU HAVE ALREADY FOOLED ME INTO DOING.

"DORJE, COME ON, I DON'T--"
"WE'LL TALK TOMORROW.
"ACTUALLY TALK.

"MAYBE FOR THE FIRST TIME EVER."

LIFE IS DIFFERENT AT ALTITUDE.
THE MOISTURE FROM YOUR BREATH TURNS THE INSIDE OF YOUR TENT INTO A FIELD OF FROST FLOWERS.
THE WHINE OF THE WIND BURNS ALL OTHER SOUNDS OUT OF HEARING RANGE.

NO! HELP ME! HELP!
WHAT'S GOING--
EXCEPT FOR SCREAMING. YOU CAN ALWAYS HEAR SCREAMING.
I THINK OF DORJE. I THINK OF HASKELL.

I IMAGINE THE WORST THING THAT COULD HAPPEN.
AND I SHOULD BE HIDING. I SHOULD BE RUNNING UP TO CAMP III.
BECAUSE WHATEVER'S COMING IS PROBABLY SO MUCH WORSE.
BUT LIKE ANY CAR CRASH, ESPECIALLY MY OWN, I CAN'T HELP BUT LOOK.

AND IT'S SO MUCH WORSE THAN I THOUGHT.
WHO EVEN KNEW THAT WAS POSSIBLE?

KATHMANDU
-2 III 93
KN-38
N.C.G.

पाँच सय

THE FIRST TIME I HANDLED A DEAD BODY, I SHOOK LIKE A LEAF.
CLIMBING, YOU GET USED TO SEEING THEM.
THE WRONG THING IS TO TREAT THEM LIKE WARNING SIGNS. OR AN OCCASION FOR SECOND THOUGHTS.
YOU LEARN TO IGNORE THEM.
UNTIL THEY BECOME SCENERY.
OR OPPORTUNITY.
I TOLD MYSELF THEY'RE DEAD--THEY DON'T CARE.
THE FIRST TIME A FAMILY PAID MADE IT EASIER.
THEY WEREN'T BODIES. THEY WERE DOLLAR SIGNS.
BUT THIS ISN'T A BODY.
COULD HAVE BEEN A HEART ATTACK OR A STROKE.
WOULD EXPLAIN THE SUDDENNESS OF IT.
MAYBE IT WAS AN EDEMA.
WE WON'T KNOW UNTIL WE GET HER BODY DOWN TO CAMP II.
THAT'LL REQUIRE FOUR OR FIVE CLIMBERS TO TURN AROUND AND HELP CARRY HER DOWN.
THIS ISN'T DEATH.
WHO'S IN?
IT'S MURDER.

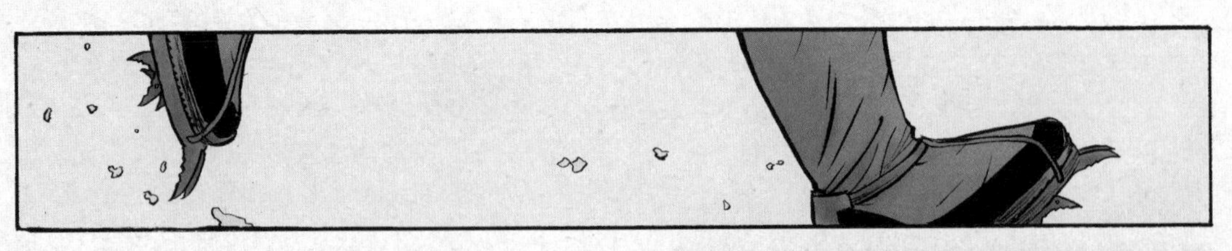

GET UP, ZAN. I'M GOING HOME.
I LEFT ALL YOUR GEAR I WAS CARRYING IN YOUR TENT. GOOD LUCK.
BLURRGGHHH!
D-DORJE... DON'T. I'LL-- I'LL TELL YOU EVERYTHING. J-JUST STAY.
TOO LATE. YOU SAID YOURSELF WE HAVE TO TRUST EACH OTHER.
AND ALL I CAN REALLY TRUST IS YOU'RE GOING TO DIE UP THERE. AND TAKE ME WITH YOU.
THANKS FOR THE FUCKING VOTE OF CONFIDENCE.
I KNOW WHAT I'M DOING. I'M NOT SOME GODDAMN AMATEUR.
COME ON, YOU'RE NOT JUST BATTLING THE MOUNTAIN. IF YOU EVER WERE.
YOU'RE INTO SOMETHING FAR, FAR WORSE.
I AM. I REALLY AM. AND I NEED YOUR HELP.
COME ON, THEN.
I'LL HELP YOU GET OUT OF HERE.
I'LL SAVE YOUR LIFE IF YOU'LL LET ME, ZAN.
PLEASE.

WE HAVE TO TAKE YOUR FRIENDS BACK DOWN.
THEN I HIKE BACK TO NAMCHE IN THE MORNING.
YOU CAN STAY WITH ME THERE. YOU CAN GO ALL THE WAY HOME.
AND WHERE THE HELL IS THAT, DORJE?
THIS IS IT FOR ME. I CAN'T GO HOME. THERE IS NO BACK.
THE SUMMIT IS MY ONLY WAY OUT.

IT'S A BARREN HUNK OF ROCK, ZAN. IT WON'T MAGICALLY FIX ALL THAT IS WRONG WITH YOU.
ESPECIALLY NOT SINCE YOU'VE BROUGHT YOUR PROBLEMS WITH YOU.
AND IT WILL ONLY GET WORSE IF YOU KEEP CLIMBING. WORSE THAN YOUR FRIENDS HERE.

I HAVE TO, DORJE. THEY HAVE MY FRIEND. I HAVE TO TRY.
NO, YOU COULD HAVE CALLED THE AUTHORITIES. IT'S NOT AS IF THEY HAVE ANYWHERE TO GO. YOU DIDN'T. BECAUSE YOU'RE HIDING. LYING. ABOUT SOMETHING.
WHO KNOWS WHO MIGHT STILL BE ALIVE IF YOU HAD JUST CALLED SOMEONE?

YOU CAN STILL TURN AROUND. SAVE YOUR OWN LIFE, IF YOU THINK YOU DESERVE IT.
THIS MOUNTAIN WILL STILL BE HERE.
THERE'S NO SHAME IN LEARNING YOUR LIMITATIONS, ZAN.
I LEARNED THEM A LONG TIME AGO, DORJE.
THAT'S WHY I'M HERE.

Three months since I quit, tried to leave it all behind, find a life.
All I found was my old one, resurfacing one job at a time.
The grisly details piled on each other. Lives taken, wounds received.
I should be haunted by the weight of what I've done, but I'm not. Not by that.
It's all the bits of loose thread and bad paint jobs when I stare close enough that bother me.
The things beneath them. All these conflicting stories.
How nothing matches up, and if one's not real, then how many dominoes fall in its wake?
Can't eat. Can't sleep. Can't breathe. I'm living in a fog of thin air and exhaustion, sickness.
Do I even exist outside the Agency?
Who's following me?
How many will they keep sending?
Only two miles left. Into the Death Zone.
Something is waiting up there for me.
Either way, I'll be prepared.

TWO OXYGEN TANKS, A RESPIRATOR, HALF A DOZEN BAGGED MEALS, TITANIUM STOVE. EVERYTHING DORJE LEFT ME.
I RECITE THE LIST OF EVERYTHING I'VE SQUEEZED INTO MY PACK. IT KEEPS MY BRAIN MOVING. DISTRACTS ME.
I DON'T THINK OF WHAT I'M LEAVING BEHIND. EVERYTHING THE AGENTS RUINED AND STOLE. ALL MY DRUGS, GONE, EXCEPT FOR THE SMALL STASH IN MY POCKET. SALVATION.
I DON'T THINK OF LAURENN OR TENZING OR THREE DEAD AGENTS.
I DON'T THINK ABOUT HASKELL'S HAND.
I FEEL THE ACHE RUNNING UP AND DOWN MY LIMBS, THE SCRATCHY HACK IN MY THROAT, MY APPETITE SHRINKING DOWN TO A KNOT.
I REGRET HOW I LAY IN MY TENT AND STARED INTO SPACE INSTEAD OF SLEEPING. HOW MY EYES ARE RAW FROM CRYING.
I GRIT MY TEETH WITH EVERY KICK OF MY CRAMPONS INTO THE GLACIER. I IGNORE THE UNHEALTHY TINGLE IN THE TIPS OF MY FINGERS.
I TELL MYSELF IT'S EVEREST. IT'S SUPPOSED TO HURT.
I'M GRATEFUL FOR THE NEXT SEVERAL HOURS OF CLIMBING.
NO MORE THINKING. JUST SURVIVING.

THERE'S THINGS THEY DON'T MENTION IN THE EXPEDITION BROCHURES. SECRETS AMONG GUIDES.
LIKE HOW, AFTER A POINT, YOU'RE MORE SCARED OF WHAT CAN HAPPEN THAN EXCITED BY WHAT WILL HAPPEN.
EXPLANATIONS OF ALL THE THINGS YOU HAVE TO SACRIFICE TO MAKE IT TO THE TOP OF A MOUNTAIN THIS HUGE.

OR HOW, TO GET TO THE SUMMIT, YOU HAVE TO STEP OFF EVEREST AND CLIMB UP THE BACK OF ITS SMALLER CONJOINED SISTER, LHOTSE. FOURTH HIGHEST PEAK IN THE WORLD.
LHOTSE IS A REAL CHALLENGE, WITH NONE OF THE GLITZ.
WHILE EVEREST IS LIKE HIKING UP A SLEDDING HILL.
THE ONLY CHALLENGE IS NOT LYING DOWN AND DYING.
ALWAYS THE BRIDESMAID.

SNOWBOARDING WAS MY LIFE. BY THE TIME I WAS 17, IT WAS A FULL-TIME JOB.
A JOB I WASN'T SURE I ENJOYED MUCH ANYMORE.
CLIMBING SEEMED HARD. AND IT WAS LITERALLY LOOMING OVER EVERY COMPETITION.

SO WHEN I WASN'T ZOOMING DOWN THE SLOPES, I HACKED MY WAY UP THEM.
IT BECAME MY SECRET THING.

EVERYTHING AT GROUND LEVEL SHIFTS TOO FAST, MOVES LIKE A RIVER.
UP HIGH, IT'S ALL MINE. I DID THIS. NO ONE TO TAKE IT AWAY. NO ONE TO BEAT ME.
NO ONE HAS TO DRAW BLOOD TO PROVE IT REALLY MATTERS.

AFTER I RAN OUT ON MY OLD LIFE I CLIMBED EVERYTHING I COULD. IT WAS MY ONLY RESPONSIBILITY.
THEN I GOT BROKE. IT BECAME A JOB. HOLDING HANDS. KEEPING THE RICH DANGER TOURISTS ALIVE.
EVERYONE FRANTIC; WEATHER WINDOWS SHRINKING, NEVER ENOUGH ROOM FOR EVERYONE'S DREAM TO FIT THROUGH IT.
NORMALLY IT'D BE MY JOB TO SOOTHE THEM, TO KEEP THEM GOING.
TO BE POLITE.
BUT I DON'T HAVE TO BE POLITE ANYMORE.
WHETHER THESE PEOPLE LIVE OR DIE ISN'T MY JOB.
LAURENN WASN'T MY JOB. TENZING WASN'T.
NOT EVEN HASKELL.

CLIMBING TEACHES YOU THAT YOU'RE ALL ALONE.

ALL YOU HAVE IS YOUR BODY AND WILLPOWER TO KEEP IT MOVING.
TO FIGHT TO GET TO SOMEWHERE HIGHER AND MORE DESOLATE.

SOUNDS FAMILIAR.
SUZANNE. SO GLAD YOU COULD JOIN US.
WE'VE BEEN WAITING.

I TOLD THE MAJOR SHE WOULDN'T LISTEN TO REASON.
SO DO WE GET RID OF PRICE NOW?

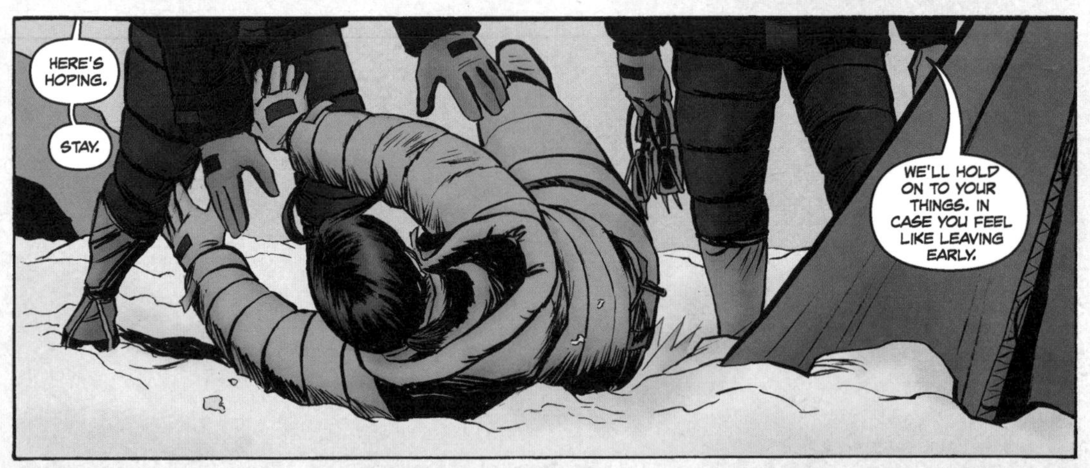
HERE'S HOPING.
STAY.
WE'LL HOLD ON TO YOUR THINGS. IN CASE YOU FEEL LIKE LEAVING EARLY.

UFF
MAKE YOURSELF COMFORTABLE, MS. JENSEN. SOMEONE WILL BE WITH YOU.

YOU IDIOT...

I DON'T KNOW WHY I THOUGHT YOU'D TURN AROUND.
I'VE ALWAYS BEEN A BIT OF A DREAMER, I GUESS.
SO, HOW ARE YOU LIKING EVEREST?

SHUT UP, HASKELL.
YEAH, I MISSED YOU TOO.

HELLO. WE FINALLY MEET.
PLEASE DON'T SPEAK. THIS WILL GO FASTER.

NO MORE CAT AND MOUSE. NO MORE THREATS.

YOU'RE OUR PRISONER, AND YOU'LL BE LEADING US UP TO THE SUMMIT.

OR WHAT? YOU KILL ME? I DON'T CARE--
IT'S CRYSTAL CLEAR YOU DON'T.

THWACK

WHICH IS WHY I'LL STAY HERE WITH YOU, FIND SOMETHING YOU DO CARE ABOUT. LIKE YOUR FINGERS OR EYES. OR YOUR PARTNER.
WE WILL FIND IT.
YOU WON'T KNOW WHAT TO DO WITH IT.
SUZANNE. STOP.

LISTEN TO HIM. HE KNOWS HOW WE WORK.
SPEAKING OF...
DID YOU BRING HIS HAND WITH? OR JUST YOUR DRUGS?

LET--LET HASKELL GO. I'LL LEAD YOU.

SORRY, THAT REMOVES THE CHALLENGE.
THINK OF IT AS A CONTEST.
WINNER LIVES.
LOSER JOINS THE OTHER BODIES UP HERE, ANOTHER FROZEN ANONYMOUS LANDMARK.
I TRUST YOU CAN APPRECIATE THE IRONY.

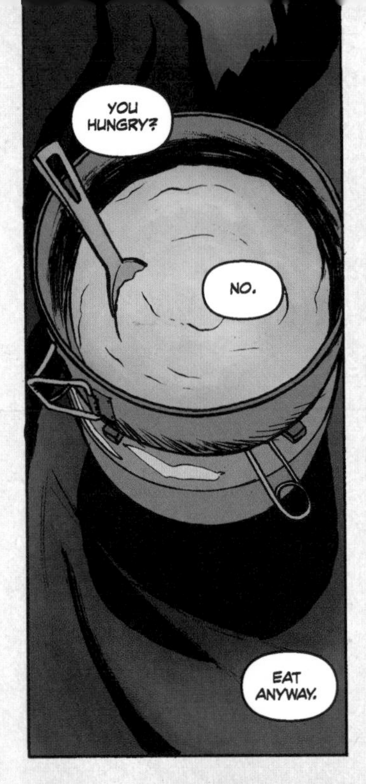
YOU HUNGRY?
NO.
EAT ANYWAY.

FOOD'S NOT GREAT, BUT THERE'S PLENTY OF IT. ALL THINGS CONSIDERED, I'VE BEEN ON WORSE CLIMBS.
HASKELL. STOP. YOU'RE FREAKING ME OUT.
STOP ACTING LIKE THIS IS NORMAL.

I'VE BEEN LIVING LIKE THIS FOR TWO WEEKS, SUZANNE. IT'S THE ONLY WAY I MANAGE TO GET ON MY FEET EVERY MORNING.
THAT AND THINKING YOU WERE SAFE.

HOW...HOW COULD I?
I HAD TO COME. AFTER WHAT THEY DID. WHAT WAS I SUPPOSED TO DO? JUST GO BACK TO MY OLD LIFE?
OR MAYBE SOMETHING NEW? YOU'RE NOT EXACTLY OUT OF OPTIONS HERE.
DAMMIT, I'VE BEEN TRYING TO SAVE YOU SINCE WE MET. JUST ONCE, I WISH YOU'D LET IT STICK.
HASKELL, YOU CAN'T SAVE ME. I KNOW YOU TRIED. EVERYONE DID.
EVERYONE BUT ME.
BESIDES, THERE ISN'T ANYTHING TO SAVE.
THE MONEY'S GONE. SO'S MY PASSPORT. I'M BACK TO FAKE NAMES AND WHATEVER I CAN CARRY.
THIS IS ALL I HAVE. ALL I NEED. GODDAMMIT, I'M GOING TO SAVE YOU THIS TIME.
YOU'RE GOING TO NEED MORE THAN THAT, THEN.

WHERE DID YOU GET IT?
IT WAS WHEN THEY WERE DIGGING US OUT FROM THE ICEFALL. I WAS PACKED TIGHT AGAINST ONE OF THEM. HIS NECK HAD SNAPPED FROM THE IMPACT.

SO I TOOK IT. OLD HABITS DIE HARD.

WHY ARE YOU JUST CARRYING IT AROUND? WHY HAVEN'T YOU USED IT?

BECAUSE I WAS NEVER PLANNING ON BREAKING LOOSE.

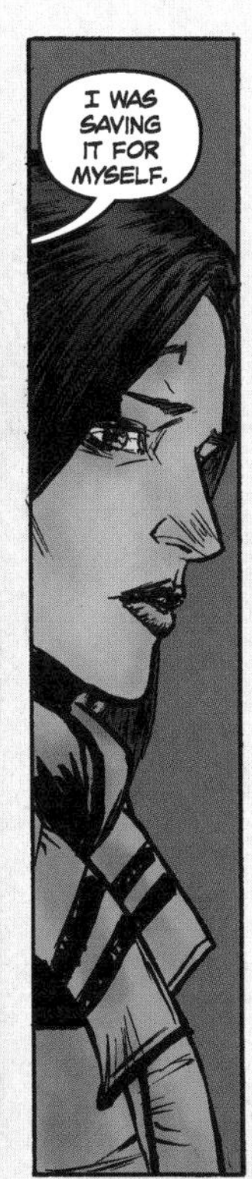
I WAS SAVING IT FOR MYSELF.

IT'S ONE BULLET. IT CAN'T DO A THING ABOUT THOSE EVIL SHITS STANDING WATCH OUT THERE. BUT IT CAN LEAVE THEM LOST, NO GUIDE AND A MESS TO EXPLAIN.
STOP. WE'RE GETTING OUT OF HERE. THIS IS THE KEY.
THAT WAS THE PLAN. UNTIL YOU SHOWED UP.

LET'S MAKE A NEW PLAN THEN.
ONE WHERE WE LIVE AND THEY DIE.
LET'S SAVE EACH OTHER.
THEN WE CAN SUMMIT. TOGETHER.

HAHA! THAT'S...
YOU'RE SERIOUS, AREN'T YOU?

WHAT ELSE DO WE DO? LIE DOWN AND DIE?
IT'S OUR INSURANCE. OUR RETIREMENT. WE CAN BOTH GET OUT OF THIS LIFE. FOR GOOD.
MARS HAS SIX MORE OF THESE IN HIM. THINK HOW MUCH THAT'S WORTH.
FINE. TELL ME YOUR MAGIC PLAN.
WE'LL TALK ABOUT WHAT COMES AFTER, IF THERE IS AN AFTER.

"IT'S SIMPLE. WE DO WHAT WE ALWAYS DO."
GET IT TOGETHER. WE MOVE OUT IN FIVE.
"YOU'RE GOING TO HAVE TO BE LESS VAGUE, SUZANNE."
"WE LIE. WE MAKE THEM THINK WE'RE HELPING THEM."
"THEN WE STICK THE KNIFE IN."
"THIS IS WHY WE WORK SO WELL TOGETHER, HASKELL."
AH, QUITE THE SAVIOR YOU ARE, SUZANNE.
"WHAT, WE'RE BOTH AMORAL SHITS?"
"AMORAL SHITS WHO UNDERSTAND EACH OTHER."

FUCK YOU, HASKELL!
I CAME HERE TO SAVE YOU AND YOU ACT LIKE AN ASSHOLE.

THEY CUT MY DAMN HAND OFF. HAVEN'T YOU DONE ENOUGH?
I'M SORRY I DID!
MAKE THEM QUIET.

I'VE GONE THROUGH HELL TO GET THIS FAR.
AND FOR WHAT? WHY THE FUCK AM I HERE?

KNOCK IT OFF. LET'S GO.

DON'T MAKE ME KILL YOU.

KEEP MOVING.

AAGHH!
GRAB HIM!

BACK OFF. I MEAN IT.
PUT YOUR GUNS DOWN OR I PUT HIM DOWN.
HONESTLY, PRICE? I THOUGHT WE'D GROWN CLOSE.

TURNS OUT YOU DON'T GET US AT ALL, DO YOU?
PFFFSST

NNG
THEY'RE BLUFFING. THEY WON'T SHOOT US!
THEY NEED US.
PAY ATTENTION, MISS JENSEN.
WE ONLY NEED ONE OF YOU.

GOODBYE, HASKELL.
GO.
FALLING IS TERRIFYING.
PFFFSST
NO ROPES, NO SAFETY CLIPS, NO TRACTION.
PFFFSST
PFFFSST
EVERYTHING MOVES IN SLOW MOTION.
ALL YOU KNOW IS YOU'RE GOING TO GET HURT.
KLIK
YOU LOSE.
PRICE!
I DON'T EVEN SCREAM.
I TUMBLE DOWN THE FACE, TRYING TO STOP MYSELF, FAILING EVERY TIME.
AS I SLIDE TOWARDS THE CREVASSE, MY LIFE DOESN'T FLASH BEFORE MY EYES.
WHAT A GODDAMN RIP-OFF.

HELP--URK--
HELP ME UP.
I'M KILLING
PRICE MYSELF.
SORRY, AGENT. YOU KNOW THE RULES.
WOUNDS DON'T HEAL THIS HIGH UP.
YOU'RE A LIABILITY NOW.
WAIT. NO. STOP. LISTEN TO ME.
IT'S BEEN AN HONOR SERVING WITH YOU.
A GRATEFUL NATION SENDS ITS REGARDS.
PFFFSST

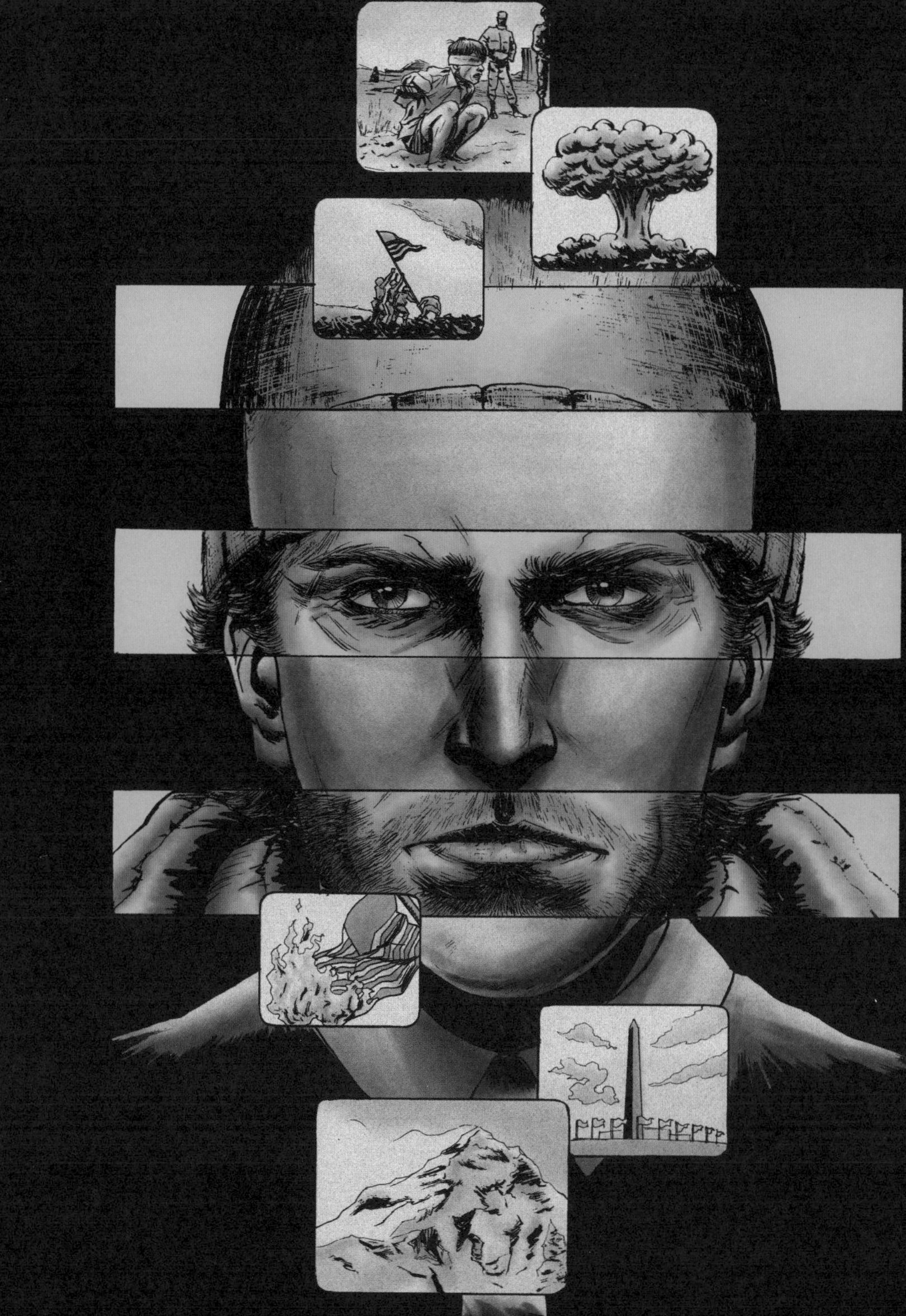

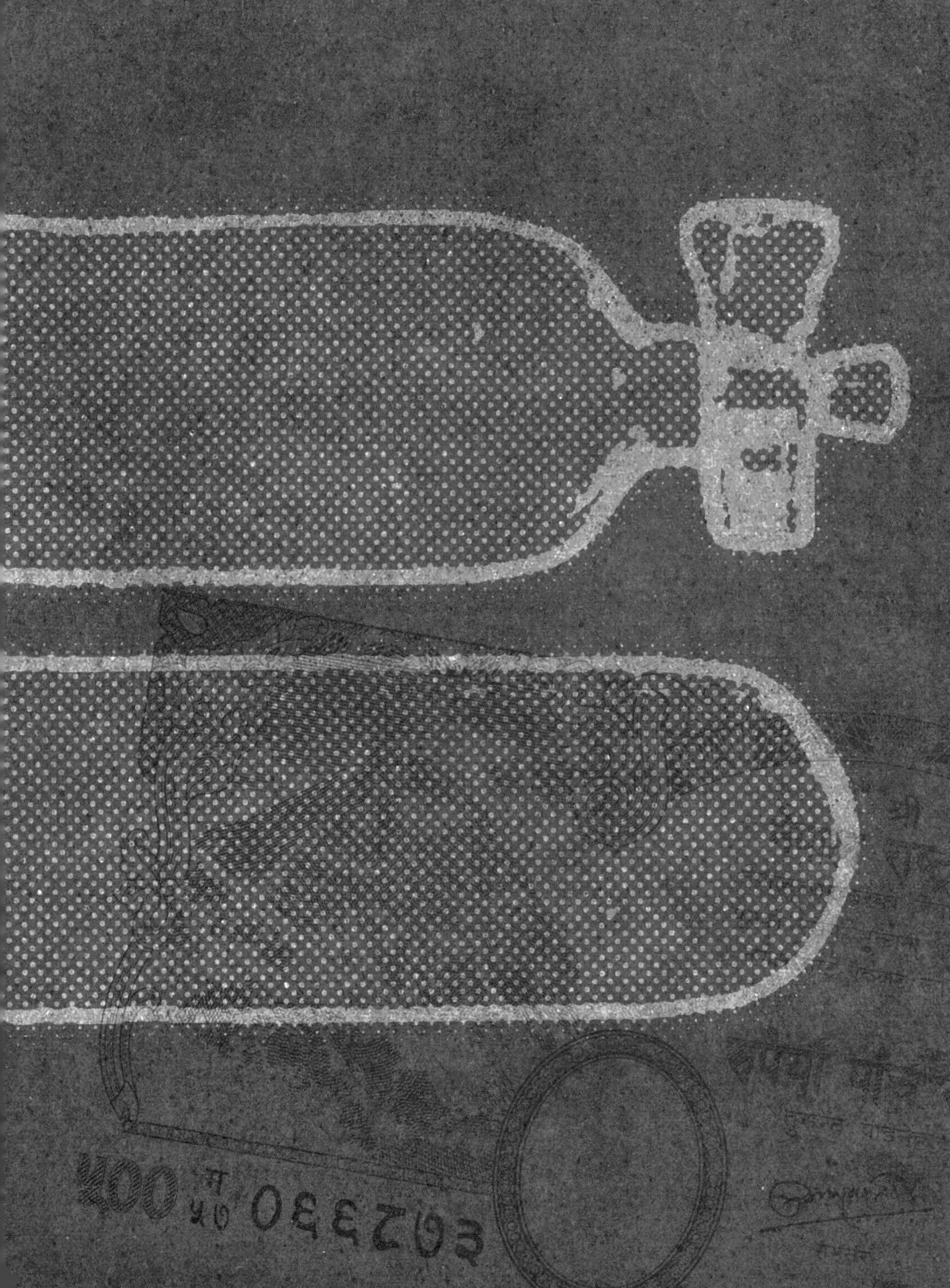

I don't think I'm going insane. Not anymore.
My mind has cleared. I see the truth now.
The Agency tried to drill my humanity out of me when I joined, but some things stick.
Like fear, doubts, rage. Like body-crippling pain.
Like memories. They tried to wipe those out too.
Replace them with something else.
But they're still there, details hidden under layers of tape and black marker.
Nothing is ever completely redacted.
I can't tell time anymore. It's been weeks, maybe months since my last dose. My last visit to the Room.
No professional friends around to interpret my hallucinations. To convince me that's what they are.
Dying isn't frightening.
Being right--that's what terrifies me.

"WELL, THAT WAS FUN.
"CALL THE MAJOR. UPDATE HIM ON THE BODY COUNT. JENSEN INCLUDED."
"ON IT."
"LET'S ROLL. WE'VE GOT...HOW MUCH FURTHER, PRICE?
"KILL ME, YOU MOTHER--UFF."
"GET UP, OLD MAN. JOB'S NOT DONE."
SHIT.
SHIT.

THERE'S 70 POUNDS OF STUFF STRAPPED TO MY BACK. EVERYTHING I NEED TO SUMMIT AND GET BACK DOWN ALIVE.

AND IT'S DRAGGING ME OFF THE WALL.

"THE PAST IS LUGGAGE."
I TRY TO REASSURE MYSELF WITH MY RULES, BUT I'M TIRED OF SHEDDING THINGS. LOSING PEOPLE.

DAMMIT.
NOT THAT I HAVE A CHOICE.
NOT THAT I EVER DID.

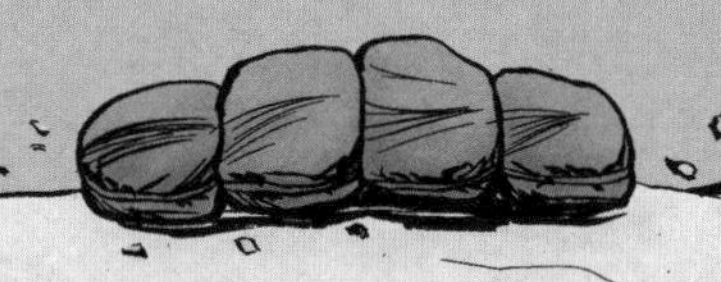
THIS IS MY ONLY CHOICE. LIVE OR DIE.
IT'S HARDER THAN YOU'D THINK SOMETIMES.

ALONE AGAIN. TRULY ALONE. NOT EVEN THE WEIGHT OF A PACK TO KEEP ME COMPANY.
MY IPOD WAS IN THAT PACK, A SOUNDTRACK OF MY LIFE BEFORE THE CRASH, NEVER UPDATED. MY PHOTOS. ME AND SOPHIE THAT NIGHT THE BAR CAUGHT FIRE. THE NECKLACE DANIEL GAVE ME ONE NIGHT WHEN WE'D BOTH HAD TOO MUCH, SAID TOO MUCH.
MY OXYGEN TANK, MY RESPIRATOR, MY CLOTHES, MY FOOD, MY TENT. ALL GONE.
I KEEP CLIMBING UP BECAUSE WHAT DOES IT MATTER NOW?
I COULD HOBBLE BACK TO CAMP III IF I'M LUCKY, BUT I'M STILL MILES FROM CIVILIZATION.
IF I DIE, I'M GONNA DIE ON MY WAY UP.
LIKE THIS UNLUCKY IDIOT.
MY CROOKED RADAR GOES OFF. SHE'S FRESH. HAS TO BE. STILL HAS BOTH OF HER HANDS.
HER BOOTS SO NEW THEY MIGHT STILL HAVE THE PRICE TAG ON THEM.
THE BAG BARELY BROKEN IN.
ANOTHER TOURIST.
SHE DOESN'T NEED IT.
THAT'S WHAT I TELL MYSELF.
THAT'S WHAT I TOLD MYSELF WITH EVERY BODY I FOUND, EVERY FAMILY WE CALLED.
I NEED THIS MORE THAN YOU.
I'LL COME BACK FOR YOU. I'LL BRING YOU HOME. FOR FREE.
NO, I WON'T.
BUT IT FEELS GOOD TO SAY. TO THINK OF SOMEONE WHO'S BEYOND PAIN FOR A MOMENT.

CAMP IV.
26,000 FEET UP.
THE DEATH ZONE.
NOT A CLEVER NICKNAME. IT'S AN OFFICIAL TERM FOR THE RAZOR-THIN ATMOSPHERE THIS HIGH UP. IT'S IN MEDICAL TEXTBOOKS. UP THIS HIGH, WITHOUT OXYGEN, THE BRAIN DIES A BIT EVERY SECOND.
AND I'VE DREAMT OF IT SO LONG, I EXPECT THE WINDS TO CARRY ME AWAY.
BUT I'M GROUNDED BY MY HUNGER--FOR OXYGEN, FOOD, FOR DRUGS--I FEEL LIKE I'M WALKING UNDERWATER.
EACH BREATH IS AGONY, EACH STEP A MONUMENTAL DECISION.
I CAN'T EVEN TELL IF I MAKE A SOUND WHEN I FALL. THE BLOOD IS POUNDING IN MY EARS.
AND IT FEELS GOOD TO LIE DOWN HERE, TO GIVE UP A LITTLE.
EVERYTHING TILL NOW HAS BEEN A DAY HIKE, A STROLL UP A HILL.
I UNDERSTAND WHAT HASKELL MEANT. ABOUT ENDURANCE. SURVIVAL.
I HEAR HIS VOICE IN MY HEAD, MUTTERING, "I TOLD YOU SO," AND IT MAKES ME FEEL BETTER. HOPEFUL.
I'LL SHOW HIM.
SURVIVING IS ALL I'VE DONE THE LAST FEW YEARS.

HELLO? ARE YOU AWAKE?
I'M ZA-- EMILY. EMILY JONES.
I GOT LOST. LOST MY TEAM.
AND MOST OF MY STUFF. OXYGEN. FOOD.
I WON'T HURT YOU. I JUST NEED SOMEWHERE TO SLEEP.
SOMEPLACE WARM. GET MY HEAD STRAIGHT. SEE WHAT I HAVE LEFT.
I TEAR THROUGH THE BAG, MY FINGERS FINALLY ABLE TO MOVE. CLOTHES, FOOD, USELESS JUNK.
OH GOD, THANK YOU.
OXYGEN. COMPLETE WITH A RIG.
I'M RICH. AGAIN.

KEEP THE SEAL CLEAN. REMEMBER WHAT DORJE TOLD ME.
I'LL LEAVE. IN THE MORNING, I SWEAR.
I ONLY NEED... I NEED SOMEONE TO HELP ME.

WILL YOU HELP ME?

PLEASE?

My father taught me to never beg for help. To stand on my own two feet and face what comes.
The war taught me nothing could harm me. That I could harm everything I set my eyes on.

The Agency taught me I was immortal. Each gray hair, every new wrinkle, they were just disguises.
After every mission we'd go into the Room. Swallow our pills, let the program swallow us.

Come out clean on the other side. All we needed to know was that we'd done something important, meaningful.
Even if it wasn't true.

We were supposed to do our jobs and forget. The program was meant to keep us from being saddled with guilt and questions.
But I never had any of either. I was grateful for the job, almost eager for it. All I ever knew well was killing.
Here, tens of thousands of miles away, it's still all I really know how to do.
No one ever taught me that. They just pointed me. Some away from it, most right towards it.
All I cared about was the quiet moments after, when all the noise went away.
Joe

All I can hear now is the wind screaming across Everest. It sounds familiar.
And I know what to do.

The further I get from my old life, I can see it wasn't a life at all, but a set of instructions.
How to be good. How to make a difference. How to fake like you are human.

Without the program, there's no more walls to compartmentalize me. I'm whole again.
And it's miserable.

I'm not a man.
I'm a monster with an off switch.
And I ran away from the only ones with access to it.

I thought I brought the war with me up here.
But there is no war. No greater good. I broke programming when it was the only thing keeping the world safe from me.

Because I was told to.
Because none of this is real.
If one part is a lie, then the rest of it comes tumbling after.
Maybe if I get to the summit...
I'll know what I'm meant to do.

MMRRR...
NO!

OH GOD. I'M SORRY, I'LL LEAVE.
I DIDN'T MEAN TO FALL ASLEEP. I WAS JUST SO--
KKKKKCCH

SSCCHHH
HEY, ARE YOU-- OH NO. HELLO?
LOOK AT ME. LOOK AT ME.
GLASSY EYED. SHALLOW BREATHS.

UNRESPONSIVE.
LOOK! I CAN FIX THIS. I CAN MAKE YOU BETTER.
I SAVED THEM FOR A REASON.
JUST STAY WITH ME.

WE'RE GOING TO MAKE IT. I'M GOING TO SAVE YOU.
I'VE BEEN CLEAN FOR DAYS NOW. THIS WAS MY "WHAT IF" STASH.

DRINK. SWALLOW. IT'S MEDICINE. IT'S GOOD FOR YOU.
YOU'RE GOING TO LIVE.
I KEPT THEM FOR MY SUMMIT PUSH, IN CASE I NEEDED TO WARD OFF THE SICKNESS FOR A FEW HOURS.

WE'RE GOING TO LIVE.
THIS IS THE LONGEST I'VE GONE IN MONTHS. YEARS MAYBE. IF I DON'T GET RID OF THEM, I WON'T BE ABLE TO RESIST.

WE'LL GET YOU HELP.
NO, WE WON'T. THERE ISN'T EVEN A "WE."
OF THE DOZEN PEOPLE CAMPED ON THIS BARREN WASTELAND UP HERE; HALF OF THEM WANT TO KILL ME AND THE OTHER HALF DON'T CARE ABOUT ANYONE BUT THEMSELVES.
MYSELF INCLUDED.

GETTING SOMEONE DOWN A MOUNTAIN ALIVE IS HARDER THAN CLIMBING UP ONE.
GETTING DEAD BODIES DOWN TAKES PLANNING. PREPARATION. EQUIPMENT. IT'S A JOB. IT'S WHY WE CHARGE SO MUCH.

IT'S WHY WE NEVER FELT BAD ABOUT WHAT WE DID.
WE RISKED OUR LIVES FOR STRANGERS. THAT'S HOW HASKELL EXPLAINED IT TO ME.
THE BODY ON THE MOUNTAIN AND THE ONES BACK HOME WAITING FOR IT. WE WERE DOING A GOOD THING, HE SAID. I REPEATED HIM EASILY.

WE WERE GIVING PEOPLE PEACE.
EVERYTHING WE DID WAS FOR THE LIVING.
BECAUSE THE LIVING ARE THE ONES WITH THE MONEY.

I CAN'T SAVE HIM, BUT I CAN TRY.
AND I'M NOT SURE WHICH HIM I MEAN ANYMORE.

WHY AREN'T WE MOVING YET?
PRICE SAYS A STORM IS ROLLING IN TONIGHT.
SAYS WE HAVE TO WAIT IT OUT.
WAIT FOR WHAT? WE'RE DYING UP HERE. I CAN'T EVEN RAISE THE MAJOR ON THE SAT PHONE ANYMORE.
AND WHY ARE WE STILL CODDLING THIS ASSHOLE? HE HELPED KILL ONE OF US.
HIM AND THAT GIRL. WHY CAN'T I RETURN THE FAVOR?
AT EASE, AGENT. JENSEN'S DEAD AT THE BOTTOM OF A DEEP, DARK HOLE. PRICE IS STILL USEFUL. HE'S BEEN UP THERE.
HE GETS US ON THE SUMMIT, WE FIND MARS, DRAG HIM DOWN, AND GO HOME. VICTORIOUS.
THE HARD PART IS ALMOST OVER. STAY ON MISSION.
BESIDES, WE'RE NOT WAITING.

"WHAT IF HE'S NOT COOPERATIVE?"
"PRICE HAS KIDS. GRANDKIDS. HE KNOWS WHAT'S AT STAKE HERE.

"IF HE LEADS US TO THE TOP, WE DO HIM QUICK, LEAVE HIM UP THERE TO REPLACE MARS.
"IF NOT, WE'RE CLOSE ENOUGH NOW THAT IT DOESN'T MATTER. HE'S ALL YOURS."
"OKAY, BUT THIS TIME YOU PACK HIS SHIT."

J.W.86
"FINE. NOW COME ON, GET EXCITED.
"WE'RE ABOUT TO SUMMIT EVEREST."

...LETTING EVERYONE KNOW THERE'S A FRONT MOVING IN. FAST. BUCKLE YOURSELVES DOWN AND JUST WAIT IT OUT.
SHOULD BE ALL CLEAR BY MORNING. EVERYONE OKAY UP THERE?
NO.

WHEN I LEFT, I LEFT EVERYTHING AND EVERYONE BEHIND.
MY PARENTS, MY BROTHER AARON, MY FRIENDS, MY NICE APARTMENT FULL OF NICE STUFF.
RECRIMINATIONS, SHAME, BEING BURNED AT THE MEDIA STAKE.

I RAN BECAUSE THEY WANTED MY MEDALS, THE THINGS I'D SACRIFICED ANY HINT OF A REAL LIFE TO EARN. THEY WERE TAINTED BY ONE LITTLE MISTAKE, BUT THEY WERE STILL MINE.
N1
Beal Feirste
BELFAST
aerphort
THEY DEFINED WHO I WAS, THESE DUMB METAL WEIGHTS. THEY TOLD ME TO RUN. THEY HELD SWAY OVER ME MORE THAN ANY DRUG EVER DID.
I WANTED TO GET RID OF THEM IN MY OWN WAY, THOUGHT LETTING GO OF THEM COULD RELEASE ME. I TRIED SO MANY TIMES.

TALL TALES
In the heart of Kathmandu
ADVENTURES
Seven Summits • Expeditions
BUT I REALIZED THEY'RE JUST THINGS. I'M STILL ME. NO MATTER WHAT I BURN OR BREAK.
I HAD TO GET RID OF ME, DROWN HER IN EVERYTHING SHE'D MISSED OUT ON. I THOUGHT THAT MIGHT WORK.
OBLITERATION ISN'T ANY EASIER THAN ESCAPE.

NOW I CAN'T RUN AWAY.
ONE MORE LAST CHANCE.
AIR
I FEEL LIKE I DID WHEN I FIRST ARRIVED IN KATHMANDU. SOBER, SCARED, ALONE.
ALL I HAD THEN WAS MY MEDALS. NOW I HAVE HASKELL, MARS, AND AN IDEA--A HOPE--THAT THE SUMMIT WILL MAKE EVERYTHING I'VE DONE SEEM WORTHWHILE.

AND YOU.
WHOEVER THE HELL YOU ARE.

COME--
≡KAFF≡
COME *ON*.
GIVE ME SOMETHING HERE.

THANKS, DORJE. AT LEAST YOU CAME THROUGH WITH ONE THING.
≡KAFF≡

WISH I HAD DRUGS.
OR ANY IDEA OF WHAT I'M DOING UP HERE ANYMORE.
JUST A VOICE, EVEN.

SOMEONE WHO CAN TALK BACK TO ME. TELL ME IT'S GOING TO BE OKAY.
SOMETHING TO DROWN OUT THE SOUND OF THIS STORM.

YOU'LL DO FOR NOW.
I CAN'T RADIO FOR HELP. THE STORM. PLUS, THE AGENTS WOULD HEAR. WE'D *BOTH* DIE.
WE'RE ALMOST THERE, STILL ALIVE.
IF YOU DON'T MIND. A LITTLE BIT LONGER.

CAN'T BREATHE.
CAN'T SEE.
I PANIC.
NEEDLES OF ICE THROUGH THE COLLAPSED TENT WALL AGAINST MY FACE.
THE WIND OUTSIDE LIKE A JET PLANE ATTACHED TO A TRAIN BEARING DOWN ON MY HEAD.
I SHOVE BACK. IT'S HEAVY, LIKE MY TENT MATE'S ARM ON ME.
MY HAND DOESN'T TREMBLE UNTIL I TAKE HIS MASK OFF.
GET UP. PLEASE, GET UP. I TRIED. I'M TRYING.
WHY... WHY IS THIS HAPPENING?
DORJE WOULD SAY IT'S BECAUSE I LIED, CHEATED, AND KILLED. ON THE BACK OF A DIVINE GODDESS.
MARS WOULD SAY IT'S THE AGENTS. THEY KNOW I'M NOT DEAD AND SABOTAGED THE TENT.
=KSSHHK= --NYONE, PLEASE RESPOND.
HASKELL WOULD SAY IT'S BECAUSE I FUCKED UP, DIDN'T PREPARE. GIVE HIS LINE ABOUT HOW ONLY FOOLS RUSH IN.
I'D SAY NOTHING, SCREAMING INSIDE, BITE MY CHEEK, MY MOUTH FULL OF BLOOD.
I'D FORGET ALL THOSE PROMISES ABOUT BEING SOMEONE BETTER, SOMEONE DIFFERENT.
I'M--I'M TRAPPED BELOW THE SUMMIT.
MY NAME IS H-H-HASKELL P-PRICE.
PLEASE. S-SOMEONE HELP ME.
I'D BE ZAN JENSEN. THE WORST POSSIBLE CHOICE OF ALL.
HE'D GIVE HIS SMIRK. NUDGE ME, ASKING, "YOU SEEN ANY FOOLS AROUND HERE?"

-2 III 93
KN-38 N.B.C.

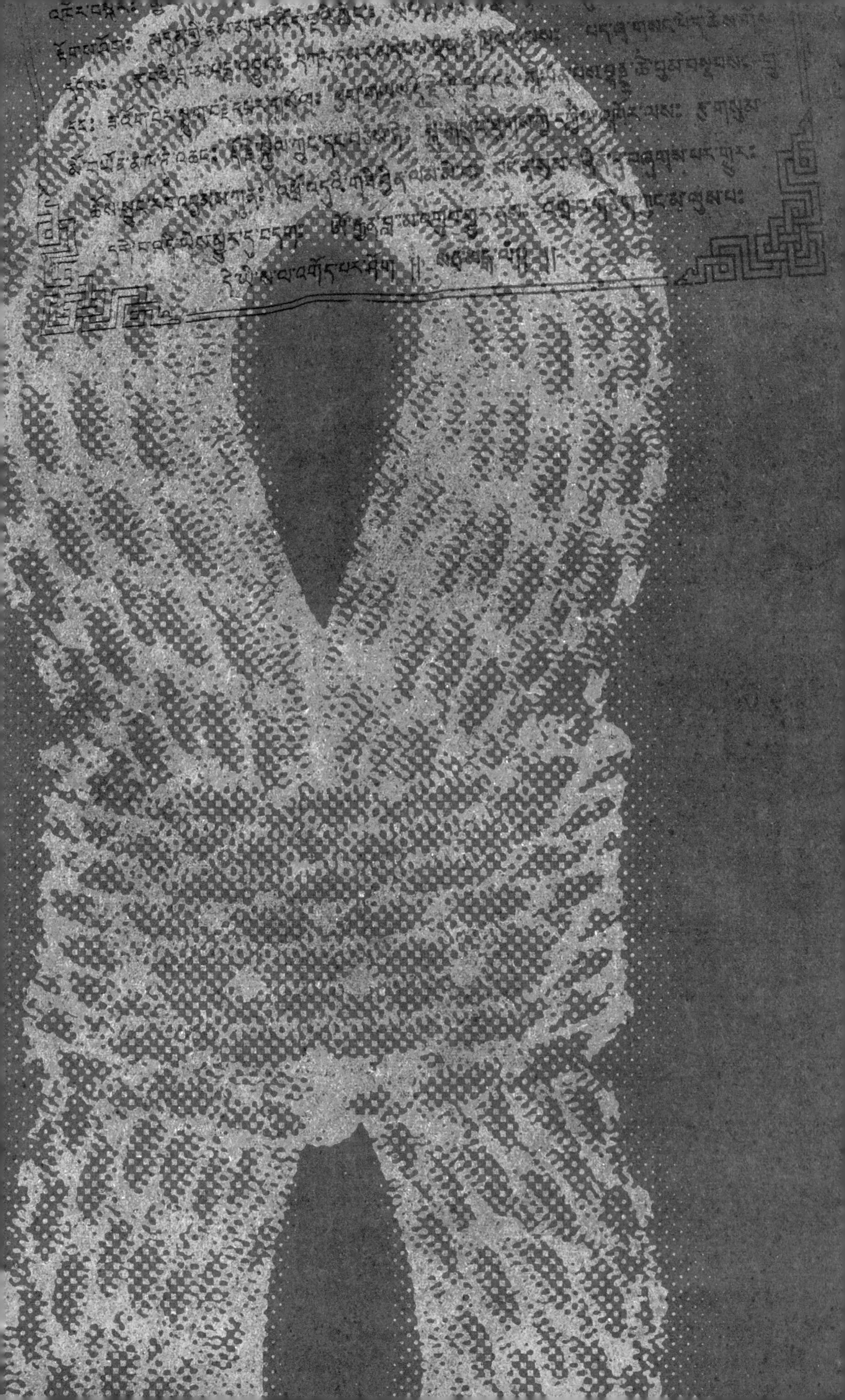

WAKE UP, GODDAMMIT.
WAKE UP.
HE'S COLD AS ICE. HIS LIMBS ARE HEAVY, HEAVIER THAN WHEN I WOKE UP WITH HIM LOCKED AROUND ME. BUT I KEEP TRYING.
TRYING TO WAKE HIM UP. TRYING NOT TO LOOK IN HIS EYES.
HE HASN'T BREATHED IN A MINUTE.
HIS JAW IS TENSE, LOCKED SHUT, LIKE TRYING TO OPEN A RUSTED WOOD STOVE.
PLEASE, GET UP. I TRIED. I'M TRYING.
DON'T THINK ABOUT HOW COLD YOU ARE.

IT'S HIS EYES THAT REALLY DO IT. SCUFFED MARBLES IN HIS HEAD THAT MEAN HE'S REALLY GONE.
MAYBE IT WAS THE COLD, OR AN EDEMA. MAYBE HE SUFFOCATED FROM THE COLLAPSED TENT BLOWING AGAINST HIS FACE ALL NIGHT.
YOU CAN'T BE DEAD. NOT NOW. I'M GOING TO SAVE YOU.
I DON'T LET IT STOP ME.

I CAN SAVE HIM, LIKE I'VE SAVED MYSELF. TIME AND AGAIN.
I CAN BRING HIM BACK. BACK FROM DEATH. DOWN THIS MOUNTAIN.

I JUST HAVE TO...
I HAVE TO LET GO.

FIRST TIME I OVERDOSED WAS IN PARIS. MAYBE THAT WAS ROME. IT WAS RIGHT AFTER MY FALL. THE MESS.
EVERYTHING WAS CALM AND DARK. THE WAY YOU HOPE IT WILL BE.

THERE WERE SO MANY BOYS. AND GIRLS. MEET THEM ONE NIGHT, CRAWL INSIDE THEIR LIVES FOR A WEEK, THEN LET THEM DRIFT AWAY.

I DON'T EVEN REMEMBER THE BOY'S NAME. HE SAVED MY LIFE. YOU'D THINK I WOULD.

LOOKING FOR SOMETHING ELSE. SOMEWHERE ELSE. SOMEONE ELSE TO BE. MOURNING MYSELF, THE ONE WHO DIED ON SOME SEEDY MATTRESS IN A SQUAT.

THE ONE WHO DIED THE MOMENT THEY KNOCKED ON MY DOOR, BLOODWORK ORDERS IN HAND.
I PLANNED HER DEATH ON THE FLY. I KNEW ALL THE DIFFERENT WAYS I COULD INJURE MYSELF IN A CRASH.

LETTING GO OF EVERYTHING IS EASY WHEN YOU HATE YOURSELF.
IT GETS ADDICTIVE.

The Agency taught me I was immortal.
They lied. They lied to all of us.
I've been hacking, spitting up blood, knifepoint migraines boring through my eyes.
The blisters on my feet started bleeding a day ago, but I can't feel my feet. My fingers are dry and cold, cracking and splitting at the tips. I don't feel them.

The adrenaline I packed is the only thing keeping me moving.
That and the truth.
I don't remember why I quit anymore.

I remember coming to Everest because I thought it would complete me, give me a fresh start, go back to the dumb kid I used to be.
But I'm dumb. I'm the one who's naive, who doesn't understand the world.
I'm a tool. A machine. They fed me my regimen. They ran me through the Room.
They ran us all through the Room.
They weren't teaching us to forget--they were teaching us to remember.

Each of us was the hero and the fallen.
Even the janitors.
Joe

EVERYTHING MOVES SLOW NOW.
I HAVE MY OXYGEN ON LOW, ENOUGH TO KEEP ME ALIVE. BUT MY BODY IS EATING ITSELF. MY BRAIN IS SHUTTING DOWN.
FWSSHHKK
TIME MOVES FAST.
--BASE CAMP ATTEMPTING ON THIS SIGNAL. IF THE CLIMBER WHO CALLED CAN HEAR ME, PLEASE RESPOND.

I HAVE TO KEEP TRACK. I HAVE THREE DAYS TOPS. I SHOULD ALREADY BE MOVING.
MY BODY WON'T OBEY. WITHDRAWAL, EXHAUSTION. I'M SWEATING BULLETS. MY LEGS COLLAPSE.
I CAN'T BE SURE ANY OF THIS IS REALLY HAPPENING.
THIS IS HASKELL PRICE. COME IN.
WHERE ARE YOU? GIVE US YOUR SITREP.
BELOW THE SUMMIT. GOT CAUGHT IN THE STORM.
INJURED MY HAND. CAN'T MOVE.

IS THERE ANYONE WITH YOU?
NO. HAD A FEW CLIMBERS I WAS WITH. BUT THEY TURNED BACK.
HELP... ME...
MATE, WITH THIS STORM BLOWING THROUGH, THE CLOSEST WE CAN GET IS CAMP II.

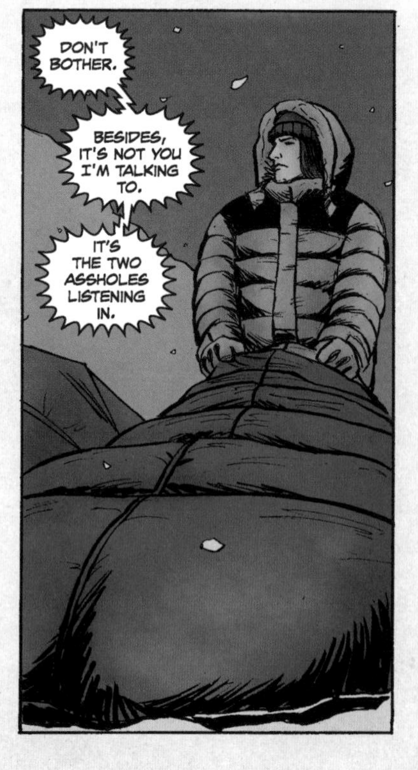
DON'T BOTHER.
BESIDES, IT'S NOT YOU I'M TALKING TO.
IT'S THE TWO ASSHOLES LISTENING IN.

WE CAN'T GET TO YOU FOR HOURS. NOW GIVE ME YOUR LOCATION.

MATE, WHAT ARE YOU--
SHUT UP. I'M GUESSING YOU CAN HEAR ME, RIGHT?
I JUST WANTED TO TELL YOU SOMETHING.
I WIN.
HASKELL PRICE. SIGNING OFF.
THIS IS...IT'S THE BEST I CAN DO.
IT'S SOMETHING PROPER.
I'LL SEND YOUR THINGS HOME. TELL THEM WHAT HAPPENED.
HOW SORRY I AM.
MAYBE THEY'LL BE PROUD.
YOU ALMOST MADE IT.
YOU TRIED SO HARD. I TRIED SO HARD.
"YOU KEPT ME ALIVE AND I COULDN'T FIX YOU.
"CAN'T FIX MYSELF."
I DON'T KNOW WHY I THOUGHT I COULD.
I'M STILL ME.
HASKELL, IT'S ZAN.
HASKELL, COME IN.

NO ONE UP HERE AT ALL. NO ONE AT ALL.
PICK UP, HASKELL. PLEASE.
TELL ME WHERE YOU ARE. TELL ME YOU'RE SAFE.
JUST ANSWER THE GODDAMN RADIO.
IS THAT REALLY YOU?
HASKELL! YES, IT'S ME. TELL ME WHERE YOU--
STOP, SUZANNE.
I DON'T WANT TO KNOW WHERE YOU ARE. I HOPE YOU'RE AT BASE CAMP. I HOPE YOU'RE RUNNING HOME.

PLEASE DON'T BE UP HERE. JUST BE ALIVE AND QUIET AND WALK THE HELL AWAY.

WHAT IF I DON'T WANT TO?
THEN YOU'RE STUPIDER THAN I EVER GAVE YOU CREDIT FOR, SUZANNE.
YOU STARTED TO BELIEVE YOUR OWN LIES.
WHAT ABOUT YOU? YOU WANT TO DIE UP THERE?

YES, GODDAMMIT. THAT'S WHAT I'VE BEEN TRYING TO TELL YOU ALL ALONG, SUZANNE.
I WAS NEVER GOING TO COME BACK DOWN. EVEN IF BY SOME MIRACLE THEY LET ME GO, I WOULD'VE DONE IT ANYWAY.
ONE SMALL MIRACLE, WE GOT SEPARATED IN THE STORM. AT LEAST NOW I GET TO CHOOSE.

"I'VE BEEN DEAD A LONG TIME.
"I CLIMB, I MAKE MONEY, I SWALLOW IT ALL AND PUT IT AWAY FOR SOME MYTHICAL DAY, AND IT'S ALL JUST A STORY I TELL MYSELF. TO FEEL BETTER. HOPING IT MIGHT MAGICALLY COME TRUE.

"THERE'S NO IOWA CITY. NO GRANDKIDS BOUNCING ON MY KNEE.
"THEY'RE GONE. I CHASED THEM AWAY. I CHASE EVERYONE AWAY AFTER ENOUGH TIME.

"EXCEPT YOU. YOU I CAN'T GET RID OF. NO MATTER HOW MUCH BETTER IT WOULD BE FOR YOU.
"NO MATTER HOW MUCH I WANT TO TURN MY BACK, I CAN'T."
THAT'S WHY WE BOTH HAVE TO GO.
I'M NOT LEAVING. THE STORM IS OVER. I'M COMING TO GET YOU, HASKELL.
SUZANNE... THEY CAN HEAR US. THE WHOLE DAMN MOUNTAIN CAN.
I KNOW THEY CAN. I DON'T GIVE A SHIT ANYMORE.

I DO. SEE, THOSE AGENTS ARE BETWEEN YOU AND ME.
IF THEY WANT TO SUMMIT, THEY CAN COME FIND ME. I DON'T WANT TO SEE YOU, SUZANNE.
KLIK
HASKELL?
HASKELL, COME IN.
This is Sullivan Mars. Strange Agent. Treasonist. Human sacrifice.
Cleanup man. Professional diversion.
Not a hero. I didn't change the world.
I watched others do it. I was only support staff.
A black-ops janitor. I cleaned up. I burned loose ends.
The Agency knew watching from the sidelines doesn't inspire a soldier.
Cleaning up a hero's mess isn't motivational.
That's what the Room is was for.
Everyone mattered in the Room.
After enough sessions, enough medication, the whole world was the Room.
I wonder if I'm still there. If this is some exercise.
If I try hard enough, can I wake up there?
Do I want to?

It doesn't hurt like I thought it would.
Makes me numb, number than the needles climbing up my fingers and toes.
None of it mattered. My whole life. Just a series of casualties, of scooped-up casings and wiped-down doorknobs.
All the bodies I've added on my way up this graveyard. Are they Agents or am I insane? Is this programming or old instincts coming out to play?
Does any of it even matter anymore?
Ever since he gave me the microfilm, told me not to go back, I've thought about it.
Even with the oxygen, I feel like I've got a plastic bag over my head. Each step is like running a mile.
I'm 300 feet and a few hours away from the summit. From my dream, the only thing I've been certain of this whole time.
This is where I'm supposed to be. I'm sure of it.

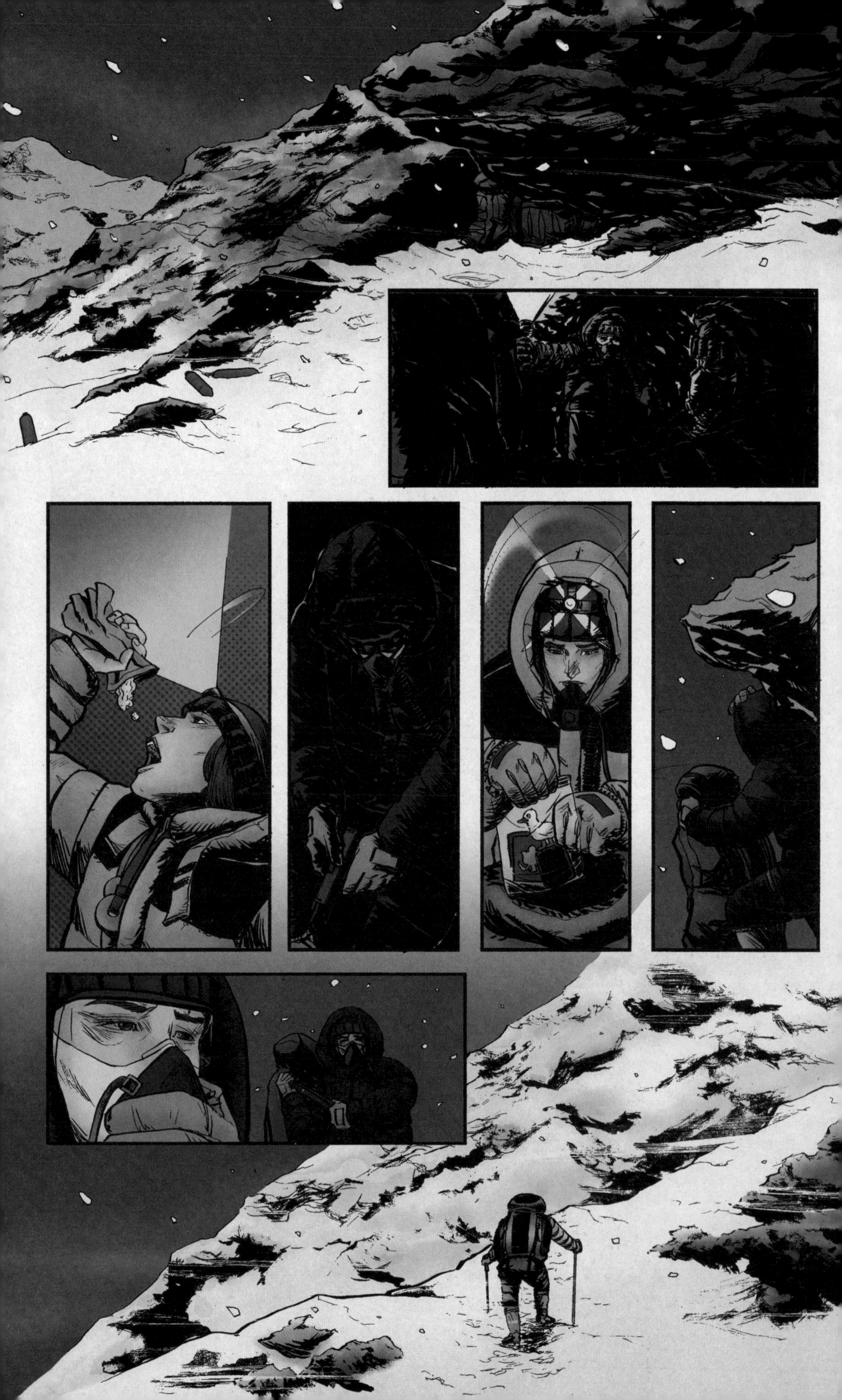

I HAVE THREE CIGARETTES LEFT.
ONE FOR ME. ONE FOR HASKELL.
ONE FOR WHEN WE GET OUT OF HERE.
I'M DONE. WITH EVERYTHING.
I'VE SWEAT THROUGH MOST OF MY DETOX. HAVEN'T HAD A DRINK SINCE BASE CAMP.
MY HEAD'S CLEAR. EACH STEP IS A KNIFE STICKING SOMEWHERE IN ME. IT KEEPS ME FOCUSED.
I SNUCK OUT OF THAT HOSPITAL INSIDE AN HOUR. THEY REFUSED TO GIVE ME DRUGS, EVEN THOUGH MY HAND WAS BROKEN.
BUT I HAD TO GO, BECAUSE OTHERWISE I'D BROKEN IT FOR NOTHING. I'D BROKEN MYSELF FOR NOTHING.

THE DOCTOR I FOUND ON MY FIRST STOP SPOKE BETTER ENGLISH THAN I DID PORTUGESE. BUT I COULD TELL FROM HIS FACE.
MY HAND NEVER FELT RIGHT AGAIN. WEAKER, CLUMSIER. USELESS FOR FINESSE; NOT THE WAY I WAS USED TO.
AND THEN THERE WAS THE PAIN.

I NEVER WAS GOOD WITH PAIN. AND THE DOCTORS I FOUND OVERSEAS WERE FAR LOOSER WITH THEIR PRESCRIPTIONS.
EVENTUALLY I FORGOT THE PAIN. FORGOT A LOT OF THINGS.

MAYBE I DESERVE TO SUFFER A LITTLE MORE.
MAYBE I'M DUE AGAIN.

HASKELL?
HASKELL, CAN YOU HEAR ME?
THIS IS YOUR PARTNER CALLING, HASKELL.
PLEASE PICK UP.
AND THIS IS OUR OFFICE. WHERE WE STORE ALL THE PERSONAL EFFECTS, WHERE WE MAKE CALLS FROM, WHERE WE TELL THEM TO MAIL THE MONEY TO.
AND WHERE YOU COME IF THINGS GO SIDEWAYS.
YOU THINK THERE'S A CHANCE OF THAT HAPPENING?
PEOPLE ARE UNPREDICTABLE. TELL THEM THE TRUTH, THEY'LL BEG FOR THE LIE. LIE, AND THEY SCREAM FOR THE TRUTH.
SQUEEZE THEM FOR MONEY, NO KNOWING WHICH WAY THEY'LL GO. THAT'S WHY I'M GIVING YOU THIS.
I DON'T-- WHAT ARE WE GETTING INTO HERE, HASKELL?
WE'RE HELPING PEOPLE, SUZANNE. FAMILIES, SPOUSES, FRIENDS--WE'RE HELPING THEM HEAL. REST. BUT MORE IMPORTANT?
WE'RE TAKING CARE OF OURSELVES. WE'RE PARTNERS. WE'RE STRONGER THAN FAMILY. WE COVER EACH OTHER'S BACKS UNTIL THE LAST MAN FALLS.
OR WOMAN.
"LET'S HOPE IT NEVER GETS TO THAT."
GOODBYE, SUZANNE.

I LOVE YOU.
HAS--
HASKELL? HASKELL!
GODDAMMIT.
HOURS TRUDGING THROUGH THE DARKNESS, HEADING TO A PLACE I'VE STUDIED FOR HOURS AND DAYS. WATCHING VIDEOS, STARING AT PHOTOS, PICTURING MYSELF STANDING THERE.
HOURS TO GO, ALL ON A DUMB BIT OF FAITH. THAT I'LL MAKE IT. THAT IT WILL BE WORTH ALL THIS.
I CAN'T TELL ANYMORE WHY I'M HERE. THE SUMMIT, MARS, HASKELL, MYSELF?
ALL I AM IS A MACHINE, PUTTING ONE FOOT I CAN'T FEEL IN FRONT OF THE OTHER, ALL OF US PACKED TOGETHER, LIKE A LOAF OF BREAD INCHING UP A HILL.
FWSSHHKK
HASKELL? WHERE HAVE YOU--
NO. YOUR PARTNER'S DEAD, JENSEN. HAVEN'T YOU BEEN PAYING ATTENTION?
NO MATTER. YOU'LL BE SET BESIDE HIS CORPSE SOON ENOUGH. NOWHERE TO RUN ANYMORE.
SEE YOU UP ON THE SUMMIT.

KATHMANDU
-2 III 33

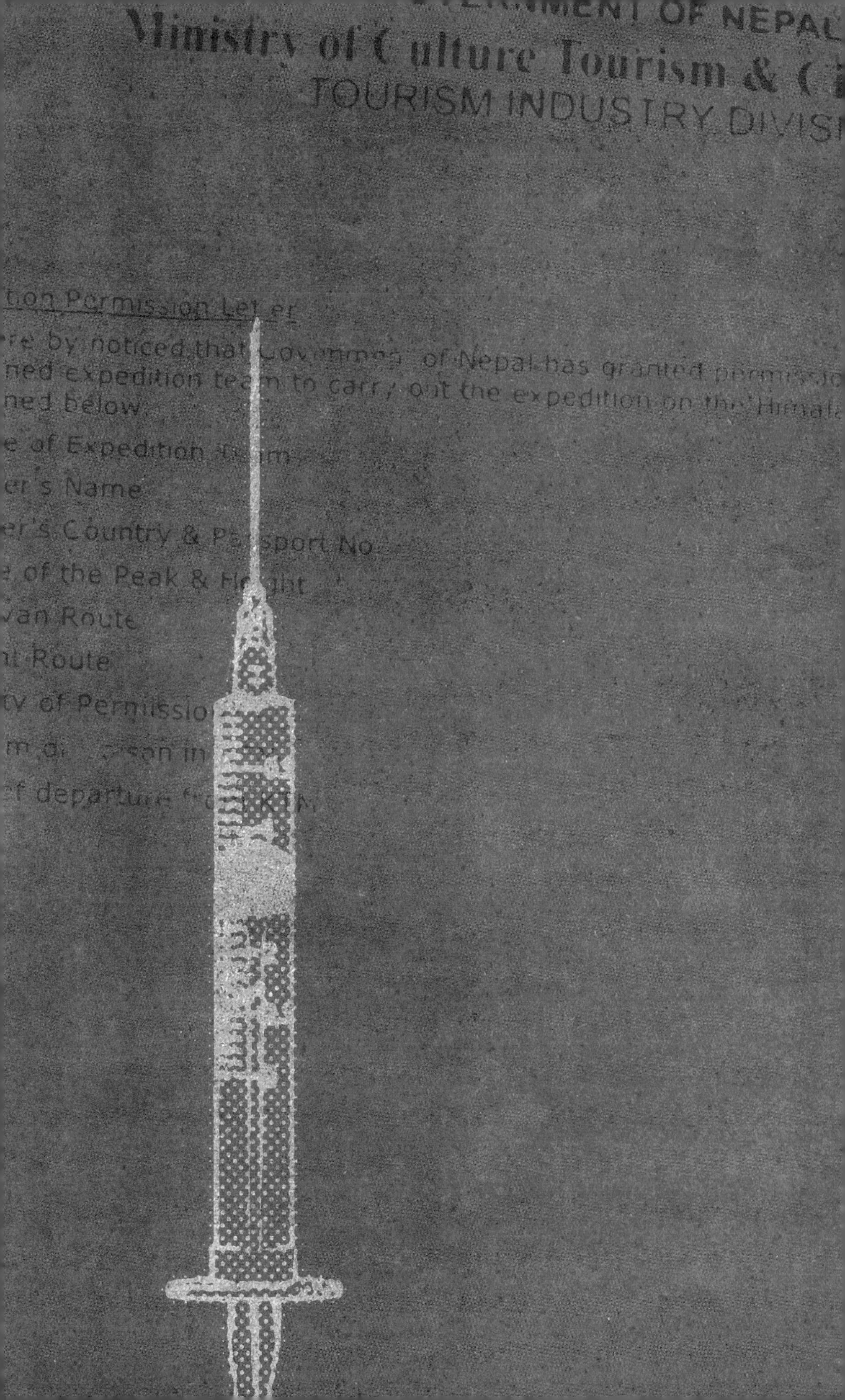

ERNMENT OF NEPAL

Ministry of Culture Tourism & C

TOURISM INDUSTRY DIVISI

tion Permission Letter

re by noticed that Governme of Nepal has granted permissio
ned expedition team to carry out the expedition on the Himal
ned below.

e of Expedition Team

er's Name

er's Country & Passport No.

e of the Peak & Height

van Route

nt Route

ty of Permissio

m d rson in

f departure from KTM

NOT EVERYTHING HURTS. SOME THINGS I CAN'T FEEL ANYMORE. MAYBE THAT'S MORE TERRIFYING.
MAYBE THIS IS WHAT DYING IS LIKE.
YOUR BODY SHUTTING DOWN SLOWLY. YOU GRIND TO A HALT. SIX OR SEVEN BREATHS BETWEEN STEPS, YOUR EYES FREEZING UP FROM THE TEARS, YOUR MOUTH DRY AS SAND.
I ALWAYS TOLD THE CLIMBERS I GUIDED TO PICK THEIR BATTLES. THAT IF THEY THOUGHT THEY WERE LOSING, THEY PROBABLY WERE.
THAT IF THEY COULD TURN AROUND UNDER THEIR OWN STEAM, THEY SHOULD.

BECAUSE ONCE YOU'RE TOO HIGH, TOO FAR, TOO WOUNDED, TOO TIRED? YOU'RE TRAPPED.
LIKE JUMPING OUT OF YOUR BOAT IN THE MIDDLE OF THE OCEAN AND SETTING IT ON FIRE.
ALL YOU HAVE LEFT IS THE JOURNEY.
THEY'D NOD, STUMBLE, KEEP MOVING FORWARD.

I KNOW HOW THEY FEEL NOW.
NO ONE WANTS TO SACRIFICE ALL THIS PAIN FOR NOTHING. FOR EMPTY POCKETS AND ENDLESS REGRETS.
WE'LL DO WHATEVER IT TAKES.
BEG, BORROW, STEAL.

THAT'S WHAT I TELL MYSELF. THEY'D DO THE SAME.
ANYONE WOULD.
AN OLD EXCUSE. IT FEELS THREADBARE, SMOOTH, WORN OUT.

STILL, IT KEEPS ME MOVING FORWARD.
THAT AND MY STOLEN OXYGEN.

A FRESH TANK ON MEDIUM MAKES THINGS FEEL EFFORTLESS. I'M WARMER, STRONGER, WIDE AWAKE. FOR THE FIRST TIME IN DAYS, I'M NOT SICK.
I TRY NOT TO REMEMBER THAT ENOUGH OXYGEN CAN GET YOU HIGH.

I RECITE MY LIST. MY NEW LIST.
SOUTH COL, BALCONY, SOUTH SUMMIT, CORNICE, HILLARY STEP, SUMMIT. I CROSS THEM OFF, CONQUERING EACH ONE.
I SAY IT OVER AND OVER.

IT'S STRANGE, BUT I FEEL GOOD. IN A WAY I HAVEN'T IN FOREVER.
I SHOULD KNOW BETTER.

THERE'S NO SUCH THING AS MIRACLES.

On the job, I never hurt, never felt anything.
Only grim satisfaction at a job well done.
The Agency bred us to be ghosts. To let go, to not care as we did these indecipherable things. They told us a story of ourselves, and we believed it.
Scar tissue brushed off me like ashes, every bad thing my hands did swirling all around me, but never touching me.
I was happy.
I followed orders. I scrubbed the blood, destroyed the bodies.
Human quicklime.
My secret was to make secrets.
Redact the real world.
Empty the dustbin of history into the fire before anyone could notice.

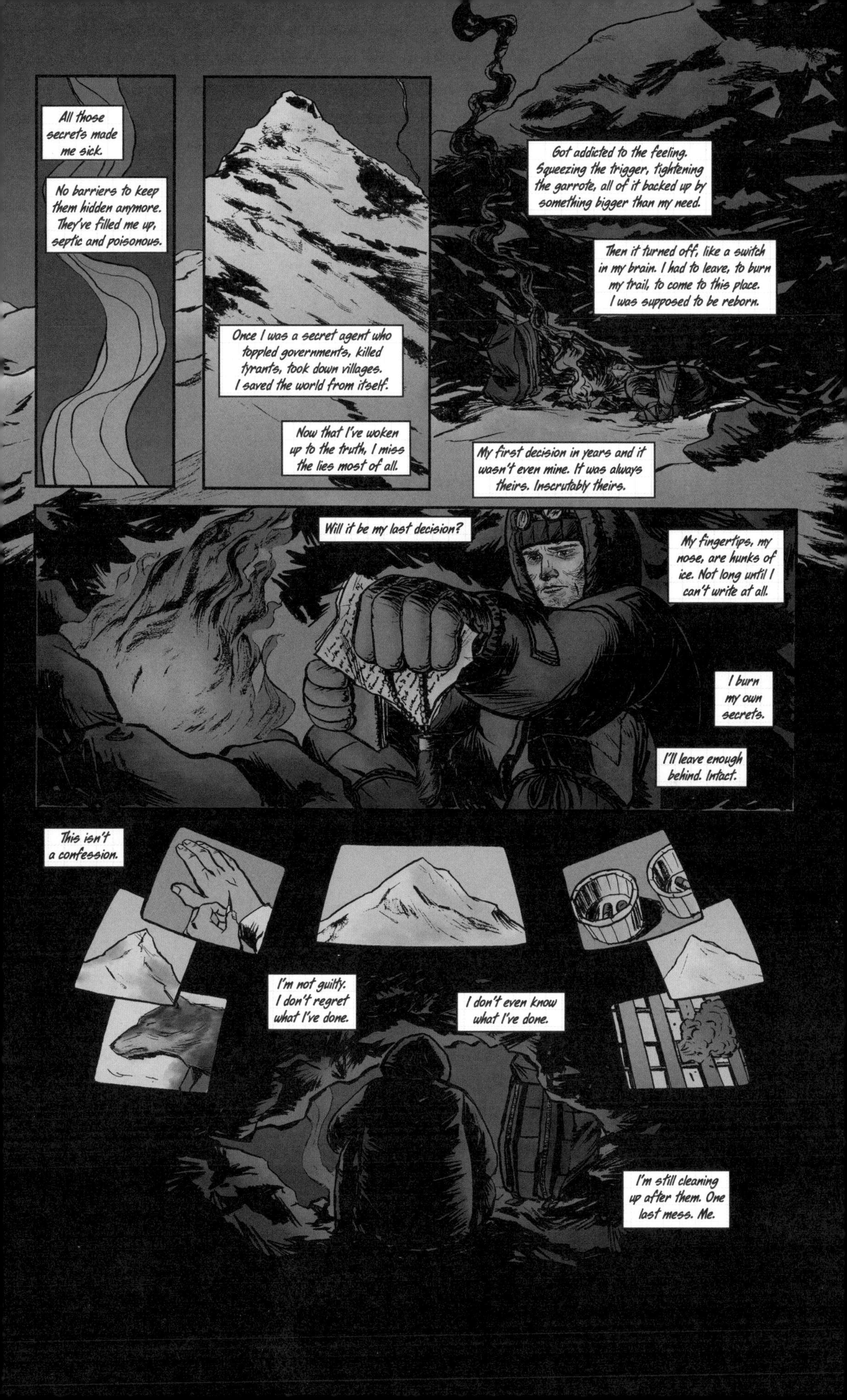

All those secrets made me sick.

No barriers to keep them hidden anymore. They've filled me up, septic and poisonous.

Once I was a secret agent who toppled governments, killed tyrants, took down villages. I saved the world from itself.

Now that I've woken up to the truth, I miss the lies most of all.

Got addicted to the feeling. Squeezing the trigger, tightening the garrote, all of it backed up by something bigger than my need.

Then it turned off, like a switch in my brain. I had to leave, to burn my trail, to come to this place. I was supposed to be reborn.

My first decision in years and it wasn't even mine. It was always theirs. Inscrutably theirs.

Will it be my last decision?

My fingertips, my nose, are hunks of ice. Not long until I can't write at all.

I burn my own secrets.

I'll leave enough behind. Intact.

This isn't a confession.

I'm not guilty. I don't regret what I've done.

I don't even know what I've done.

I'm still cleaning up after them. One last mess. Me.

HASKELL?
SAY SOMETHING.
ANYTHING.

WAKE UP.
YOU CAN'T BE--
YOU'RE NOT SUPPOSED TO--
HASKELL.

REMEMBER WHEN WE MET? YOU WERE SUCH A JERK TO ME.
YOU REMINDED ME OF MY DAD. Y'KNOW, EXCEPT BETTER.
YOU DIDN'T EXPECT ANYTHING FROM ME. YOU WEREN'T DISAPPOINTED IN ME YET.

I WOULDN'T EVEN BE ALIVE IF IT WASN'T FOR YOU. YOU LITERALLY SAVED MY LIFE. MORE THAN ONCE.
DON'T YOU WISH YOU HADN'T, NOW? JUST LEFT THE JUNKIE WHERE YOU FOUND HER?
YOU WOULD STILL BE...

I'm alive. Alive enough to keep moving. And I get it now.
I'm still following programming. Bone deep. My body blocks out the warning signs, taking me to the top, because that's where they want me to end up.
I'm a time capsule. A canary without a coal mine. Sent to die here. In as far and remote a place as possible.
Every urge some clever analyst's suggestion-box winner.
Complete with ticking clock and time bomb.
FULL
O_2
Every climber I killed just a random stash of supplies, another living rung.
Getting me high enough up that I couldn't turn back.
To trap me at the summit for future reference. Future use.
One less Agent they have to scrub out of the books.
The obedient rebel. The prodigal son.
The microfilm isn't my insurance. It's theirs.
I'm theirs. And I wish I could stop. Turn around.

GODDAMMIT, HASKELL.
THIS IS YOUR FAULT TOO.
YOUR AMAZING SCHEME. YOU WANTED TO BE SOME KIND OF RETIRED CRIMINAL MASTERMIND. "NO ONE GETS HURT," YOU SAID.
WHY? WHAT THE HELL DID ALL THIS GET YOU?

EMPTY APARTMENT, MEMENTOS, PAPERS. ALL THAT MONEY BURNED UP, GIVEN AWAY.
EVERYTHING, GONE. BECAUSE YOU HAD TO...WHY DID YOU DO IT, HASKELL? WHY DID YOU DRAG ME INTO THIS?

WHY DID I GO SO WILLINGLY?

WHAT THE HELL IS WRONG WITH US?
WHY ARE WE SO FUCKING BROKEN?

COULDN'T RESIST GETTING IN THE LAST WORD, HUH?
I LOVE YOU, YOU ASSHOLE.

AND I MEAN IT. AND I WANT TO SHATTER TO BITS FROM HOW TRUE IT ALL IS.
AND I WANT TO DIE, BUT HASKELL DOESN'T WANT THAT.
SO FOR ONCE, I LISTEN TO HIM.

I never flinched.
No matter how crazy.
I did what I had to.
Because I had to.
Because it had to be for something.
I couldn't just be a common psychopath.
I had to be great.
I try to remember that peace I felt when I decided to quit. The quiet I'd never found so easy.
This world, the only one I'd felt a part of, was dead now. The little I could make out as I left, it sounded like jealousy.
Anger.
Because I was special. Chosen.
Because I knew where I was going. I knew I was free. I saw something new, for the first time ever.
Before that last mission, before I buried every dirty operation in my body, I could see Everest.
Like I'd remembered my salvation. A home.
It still might be. Whatever's up there.

I DON'T BOTHER TO THINK ANYMORE.
EVERYTHING HURTS. EVEN MY THOUGHTS.
ESPECIALLY MY THOUGHTS.
IT'S NOTHING BUT WIND AND VOICES DROWNED OUT BY IT.
I HEAR THEM BUT I DON'T.
GETTING LATE, MISSY. MIGHT WANT TO TURN AROUND OR YOU'LL BE IN TROUBLE.
I CAN'T TURN AROUND. NOT THIS CLOSE.
I'M GOING TO SEE IT. TOUCH IT. I'M GOING TO DANCE ON IT.
THEN I'LL COLLECT MY PRIZE. THE ONLY THING I HAVE LEFT. MARS'S SECRETS.
THOSE ARE WORTH ENOUGH MONEY TO START AGAIN.
TO KEEP MYSELF SAFE FROM THEM.
TO MAKE THEM PAY.
THE STRANGE AGENTS. WHO ARE SOMEWHERE UP ABOVE ME NOW.
TOURISTS. LIKE EVERY RICH, OBLIVIOUS ASSHOLE WHOSE HAND I HELD.
THEY HAVEN'T WORKED FOR IT. HAVEN'T SUFFERED ENOUGH TO DESERVE IT.
ENTITLED. LIKE THEY DESERVE TO GET TO MARS. EXPECTING EVEREST TO BE SERVED ON A PLATE TO THEM.
NOT THIS TIME. NOT THEM.

I left home looking for a difference from my murderous heartland.
Only to discover what little I knew of real savagery.
I'd seen the world's ugliness up close. I wasn't the wolf--I was the lamb.

I hid in a double-breasted suit of armor. Traveled the world, hardly ever looking past my blinders.

Every Agent I scrubbed after their mission was me. I was too weak and afraid to turn it inward. Easier to blame the programming. The Room.
Each of us thinking we were changing the world as we helped burn it down to the foundations.
Maybe there are no conspiracies. No black ops. Maybe the only secret is that blood doesn't need a reason.

Or that there's another world.

And it's no better than the one we sacrificed everything to reach.

Suzanne. I hope you never read this.
I hope you're home. Wherever that is. I hope you've forgotten about me, about our friend tucked away on the summit.
But you are reading this, so I hope you turn around.
Please go back. They'll take you back. Nothing is as bad as this life.

You'll never get away from who you were.
Because that's who you still are. Every bad decision, every slip on the ladder, it can't be outrun.
I've tried. I'm telling you to stop.
You're mean as hell, you play dirty if it means a win, but the slightest jab and you give up so goddamn easy.

Someone stole your fight from you. That's on them.
But you stole yourself from you. That's on you, Suzanne.
Everything I ever said to you? You're my grandkids. You're my Iowa farm.

You're better than you'd ever admit. So let me do it for you.
You're Suzanne Jensen. You kicked the world's ass once. The only one keeping you from doing it again is you.

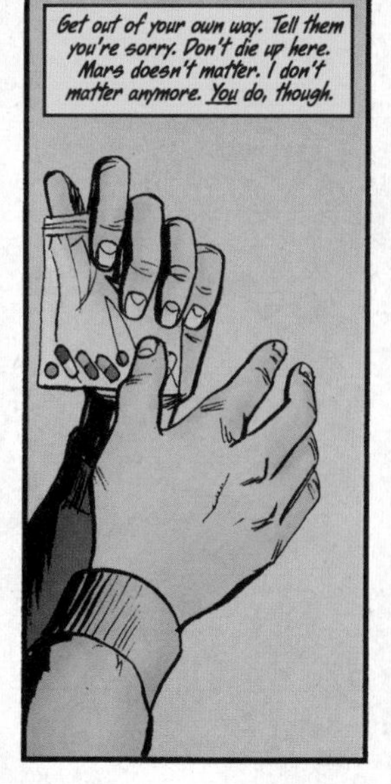
Get out of your own way. Tell them you're sorry. Don't die up here. Mars doesn't matter. I don't matter anymore. You do, though.

Stop giving up.
Now get the hell home. That's my final wish.
You have to honor it. That's the only perk of being dead.

HEY, YOU OKAY? YOU HERE ALONE?
WHAT?
WHERE IS IT?
THE SUMMIT.

RIGHT BEHIND ME, MA'AM.

YOU NEED HELP GETTING UP THERE? YOU LOOK A LITTLE UNSTEADY.
CAN YOU TURN UP MY OXYGEN? ALL THE WAY.
I'VE GOT YOU.
HERE, GRAB ON TO ME. I'LL GET YOU THERE.
NO.
THANKS. YOU GO.

I'VE GOT THIS ONE.
I--I C-C-AN'T-- WH-WHERE IS HE S-S-SUPPOSED TO BE BURIED?
HE'S HERE. FIND HIM. WE DON'T HAVE MUCH TIME.

WHERE THE HELL IS JENSEN ANYWAY?

I'm not coming back.
I know that now.
I think I always did.
And that's why I ran so blindly up this mountain.
This is my salvation.
This is what Everest does.
She waits. Tempts you.
Gives you faith.
Then shows you how wrong you were.
It'll be a kind death. Kinder than any I've ever delivered.
I don't deserve it. But none of us gets what we deserve.
They say your life flashes before your eyes when you die.
I just want to be somewhere I can look beyond my life.
To fill up the blanks with something, anything else. Even if it's another lie.

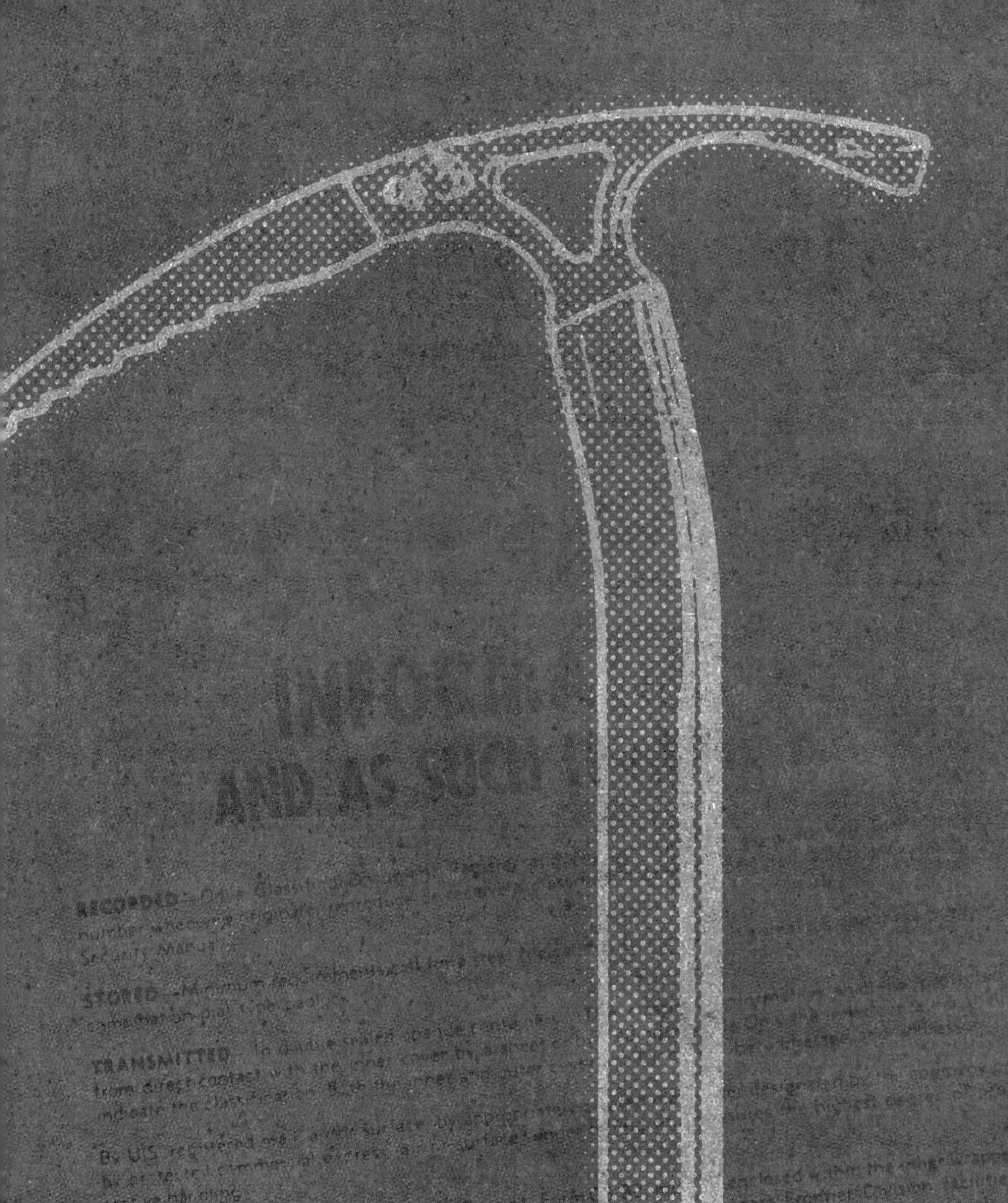

NO MORE SECOND THOUGHTS.
NO MORE WISHING.
I'M GOING TO DO WHAT I ALWAYS SHOULD'VE DONE.

FINISH SOMETHING.
I'M NOT TAKING A DIVE ANYMORE.
FOR ANYTHING.

I'D RATHER LIVE ON MY FEET THAN DIE ON MY--
T-TAG HER.

NO.
I DON'T WANT TO DIE.
BANG
BANG
NOT UP HERE. NOT WITH THEM.

NOT EVER. I WANT TO LIVE. I NEED MORE TIME.
TIME ENOUGH TO FIX ALL THIS.

WHERE IS SULLIVAN MARS?
PRICE KNEW. YOU KNOW. TELL US AND WE CAN END THIS.
I-I DON'T KN-KNOW. HE DIDN'T DRAW ME A MAP BEFORE YOU KILLED HIM.

YOU'RE JUST FULL OF BAD LUCK THEN.
IF THERE'S NO BODY ON THE SUMMIT, THEN WE'LL HAVE TO LEAVE ONE.

I'M S-SO CLOSE. JUST LET ME SEE IT. LET ME TOUCH THE GODDAMN SUMMIT.
THEN YOU CAN DO WHAT YOU LIKE.

WE DON'T NEED YOUR PERMISSION, JENSEN. FIND MARS. *NOW.*

I CAN'T... CAN'T B-- BREATHE.
WHEN I WAS A KID, I GREW UP ON A FARM.
WE HAD A WOLF ALWAYS COMING AROUND, KILLING OUR LIVESTOCK.
MY FATHER TOOK ME HUNTING. HANDED ME THE GUN, POINTED AT THE WOLF, AND SAID, "DO IT."

WHAT DO YOU THINK I DID?

FUNNY. I HAVE A STORY JUST LIKE THAT.
ONLY IT'S MY-- GODDAMMIT. OXYGEN'S OUT.
CALL THE MAJOR.
BUT WE COULDN'T GET A SIGNAL LAST--

CALL HIM OR I'LL *THROW YOU* OFF THIS MOUNTAIN.
CALM DOWN, AGENT.

HE'S ON.

GIVE IT TO *HER.*

DECISION TIME, JENSEN. THIS ISN'T ONLY YOUR LIFE YOU'RE FLUSHING AWAY ANYMORE.
WE HAVE FILES ON YOUR FAMILY. EVERY FRIEND, FORMER FRIEND, AND TEAMMATE YOU'VE EVER HAD. EVERYONE YOU'VE EVER SLEPT WITH.
WE'LL BURN YOUR LIFE TO THE GROUND, EVEN IF YOU'RE NOT LIVING IN IT ANYMORE.

I'LL STILL HAVE YOUR SECRETS.
SEND EVERYONE YOU WANT. THEY'LL NEVER FIND MARS, EVEN IF THEY MANAGE TO GET UP HERE. OR BACK DOWN.
AND DO WHAT WITH THEM? TRY TO SELL THEM, MAIL COPIES TO JOURNALISTS? THIS ISN'T 20 YEARS AGO. WE HAVE OUR EYES ON EVERYTHING NOW.

FINE, MISS JENSEN. TAKE MY MEN TO MARS'S BODY AND THEY'LL LET YOU GO.
I'LL GIVE YOU A FRESH START. I CAN WIPE YOUR SLATE CLEAN.
WE'LL TALK WHEN I'M BACK IN KATHMANDU. WHEN I'M DANCING ON YOUR GRAVE.
NO. WE WON'T. WE'RE DONE TALKING. GOODBYE.

SOUNDS LIKE YOUR NEGOTIATIONS WENT BADLY.
YOU WON'T BE NEEDING THAT OXYGEN THEN.

LET'S MAKE A DEAL. AN EXCHANGE.
LET ME TOUCH THE SUMMIT AND I GIVE YOU THE TANK.
I'LL TELL YOU WHERE MARS IS.
OR WE SHOOT YOU AND TAKE IT.
CAN YOU SHOOT ME BEFORE I THROW IT?
WILL YOU TWO GET DOWN FROM HERE WITHOUT OXYGEN?
YOU'RE NOT IMMORTAL. MAYBE ALL THE PILLS THEY PUT YOU ON, YOUR SESSIONS IN THE ROOM SAY OTHERWISE.

BUT WE ALL DIE IF I DON'T GET UP THERE.
HOW DO YOU...
I'LL GIVE YOU MARS, MY TANK, AND ANOTHER FULL ONE I LEFT JUST BELOW THE STEP. THEN YOU CAN PUT ME OUT OF ALL OF OUR MISERIES.
IT'S NOT LIKE THERE'S ANYWHERE TO RUN TO.
NOT WITH US BEHIND YOU. MOVE.
THERE'S NO WAY TO PROPERLY PREPARE FOR YOUR DREAMS COMING TRUE.
EVEN WHEN IT'S ALL YOU'VE BEEN WORKING TOWARDS AS LONG AS YOU CAN REMEMBER ANYMORE.
THE REALLY SCARY PART IS THE NEXT THING YOU THINK.
NOW WHAT?

I'VE BEEN CLIMBING SO LONG, IT TAKES A SECOND TO DEAL WITH THE IDEA THAT THERE'S NOTHING LEFT TO CLIMB.
ANOTHER TO LOOK AROUND AND RECOGNIZE THAT I'M ON THE SUMMIT.
AND I'M ABOUT TO DIE.
SO MANY THINGS GO THROUGH YOUR HEAD.
I'VE ALREADY SPENT TOO MUCH TIME THIS HIGH UP. NO OXYGEN; NO CAUTION. I'M GOING TO DIE ANYWAY.
OKAY, JENSEN, YOU SAW IT. WE'RE MOVING. NOW.
GIVE ME YOUR OXYGEN.

CLIMBING IS ABOUT PLANNING. A WAY UP IS ONLY HALF OF IT. YOU NEED A WAY DOWN.
EVEN A ROUGH IDEA.

ALL I REMEMBER IS WHAT NOT TO DO ANYMORE.
FROM MY PARENTS; MY COACH; FROM HASKELL AND SOPHIE AND...FROM DORJE.

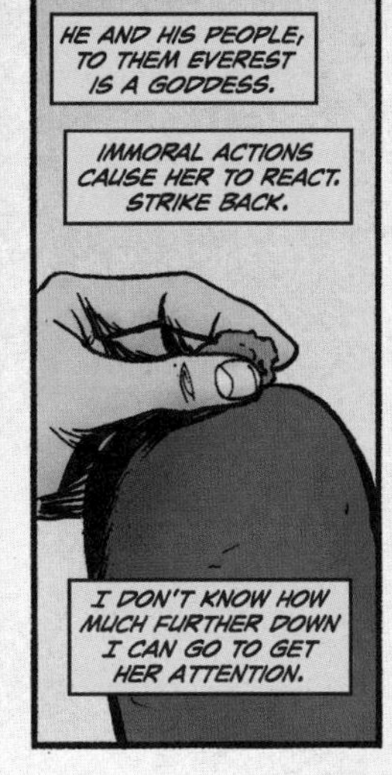
HE AND HIS PEOPLE; TO THEM EVEREST IS A GODDESS.
IMMORAL ACTIONS CAUSE HER TO REACT. STRIKE BACK.
I DON'T KNOW HOW MUCH FURTHER DOWN I CAN GO TO GET HER ATTENTION.

HERE. TAKE IT.
NOW WHERE'S MARS?
AND WHERE'S THAT OTHER TANK?

I TAKE IT ALL IN ONE LAST TIME. THE GOOD AND BAD.
I HOPE SHE'S LISTENING.
I DON'T KNOW.
THEN YOU'RE DEAD.

I KNOW. I HAVE KNOWN.
AND SO IS ONE OF YOU, UNLESS YOU SHARE THAT LITTLE TANK.
YOU'LL HAVE TO GET DOWN TO CAMP III. IN THE DARK. WITHOUT OXYGEN. WITHOUT A GUIDE.
LOOKING OUT FOR EACH OTHER WHILE YOUR BRAINS STARVE FOR OXYGEN.
DO YOU EVEN KNOW EACH OTHER'S NAMES?
THE AGENTS AREN'T GODS.
GIVE ME THAT TANK, AGENT!
NOT UNTIL YOU CALM DOWN!
THEY'RE STILL PEOPLE.
GREED, FEAR, SELF-PRESERVATION.
YOU CAN'T CUT THAT PART OUT.

IT'S MINE!
JENSEN!
I FALL. AGAIN.
I'VE GOTTEN GOOD AT IT.
YOU KNOW THE RULES. NO DEAD WEIGHT.
DON'T... YOU DARE.
ALMOST AS GOOD AS I AM AT RUNNING.

FOR THE FIRST TIME IN FOREVER, I'M NOT THINKING ABOUT ANYTHING.

EVERYTHING IS QUIET.

ME AND SULLIVAN MARS.
HI, SULLIVAN.
HE SEEMED EVEN LESS REAL THAN THE SUMMIT.
I TOUCH HIM TO MAKE SURE.
HIS MISSING HAND. ALL CURLED UP ON HIMSELF.
CURLING HIMSELF AROUND THE LAST BITS OF WARMTH.
I KNOW THE FEELING.
I HAVEN'T HAD OXYGEN IN WHAT FEELS LIKE A DAY.
IT WOULD BE SO SIMPLE TO JUST CRAWL OUT OF THE WIND AND SLEEP. BUT I HAVE PROMISES TO KEEP. THE FIRST ONES IN A WHILE.

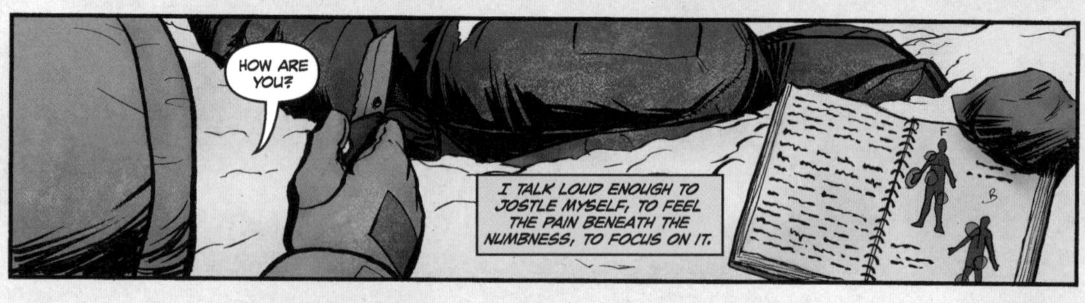
HOW ARE YOU?
I TALK LOUD ENOUGH TO JOSTLE MYSELF, TO FEEL THE PAIN BENEATH THE NUMBNESS, TO FOCUS ON IT.

I MADE IT. LIKE I SAID I WOULD. I GOT TO YOU.
SOMEONE GAVE A SHIT, SULLIVAN.
I CAME TO DO WHAT YOU COULDN'T.
YOU'RE STILL GOING TO SAVE THE WORLD.

WE BOTH ARE.
I'M... I'M SORRY ABOUT THIS.

I REALIZED AFTER I FINISHED YOUR JOURNAL, THERE'S SO MUCH MISSING. PAGES GONE, TORN OUT.

YOU KEPT YOUR SECRETS SAFE. UP THROUGH THE END.
I'M TAKING THEM NOW, SULLIVAN.
GONNA BUY MYSELF A NEW LIFE WITH THEM.

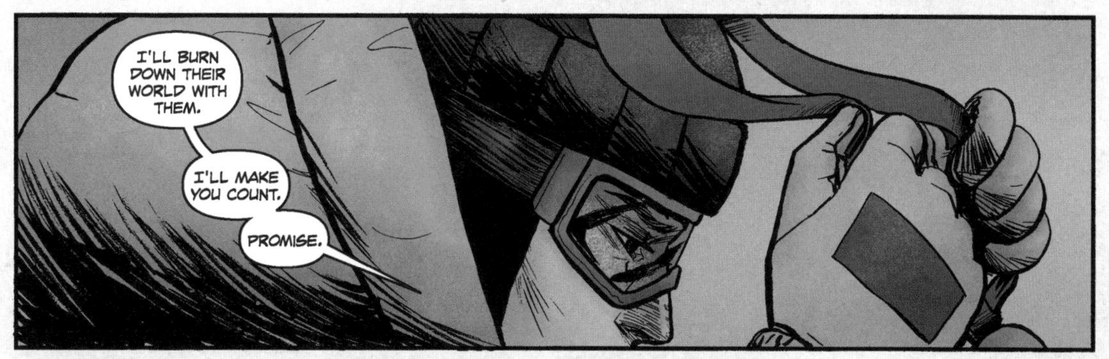
I'LL BURN DOWN THEIR WORLD WITH THEM.
I'LL MAKE YOU COUNT.
PROMISE.

I THINK IF YOU'D MADE IT BACK, YOU WOULD'VE BEEN CHANGED.
GONE ON TO LIVE SOME LIFE YOU COULD STAND TO REMEMBER.

GLORIOUSLY DULL AND NORMAL.
TELLING WAR STORIES, WHERE YOU'RE ALWAYS THE HERO.
YOU ARE. FOR ME, YOU ARE.
HOW FUCKED UP IS THAT?

THE FIRST THING YOU LEARN WHEN CLIMBING IS WHEN TO SAY WHEN.
TO KNOW YOUR LIMITS, TO KNOW WHEN YOU'VE GONE TOO FAR, EXPENDED TOO MUCH ENERGY.
WHEN THINGS GET DANGEROUS.
I DID IT.
I FUCKING DID IT.
YOU THINK, ALL I NEED IS ENOUGH TO GET THERE.
GOING UP IS ALWAYS HARDER THAN COMING DOWN. THAT'S CONVENTIONAL LOGIC.
NOT HERE AT ALTITUDE.
GETTING TO THE TOP IS ALMOST IMPOSSIBLE. EVERYTHING TELLING YOU TO TURN AROUND.
BUT WHEN THAT PART IS OVER, GETTING BACK DOWN, ALIVE, BACK TO NORMAL...
THAT'S THE HARD PART.

"--SIX WEEKS SINCE THE CONCLUSION OF CLIMBING SEASON ON EVEREST, WHICH IS STILL SHROUDED IN--
"--ONE OF THE DEADLIEST SEASONS IN RECENT MEMORY. SEVERAL CONFLICTING REPORTS HAVE SPARKED INTERNATIONAL CONTROVERSY AND DEBATE--
"--TOLL INCLUDES SEVERAL AMERICAN CITIZENS, PROMPTING THE DEPARTMENT OF STATE TO SEND REPRESENTATIVES TO NEPAL FOR A FULL ACCOUNTING--"
WE'RE MERELY HERE TO ASSIST IN ASCERTAINING THE TRUTH OF THESE REPORTS.
TO BRING PEACE OF MIND TO THE FAMILIES WHO HAVE LOST LOVED ONES.
WE'LL REMAIN HERE IN NEPAL-- IN *KATHMANDU*-- FOR AS LONG AS IT TAKES.
THAT'S ENOUGH.
WHO IS THAT, ZAN?
NO ONE. JUST THOUGHT I RECOGNIZED HIS VOICE. HAD TO MAKE SURE.
THANKS, SOPHIE.
YOU OKAY TODAY, GIRL? YOU SEEM MORE OUT OF IT THAN USUAL.
IT'S THE MEDICATION I'M ON. MAKES ME A LITTLE LOOPY.
I'M GREAT.
OKAY.
'CAUSE YOU KNOW, YOU CAN ALWAYS--
I SHOULD GO.

DON'T GO. STAY HERE. WE'LL GET SOME FOOD. YOU CAN COME CRASH AT MY PLACE.
OR WE CAN GO SOMEWHERE! HOW DO YOU FEEL ABOUT VIENNA? MY TREAT!
UNLESS YOU'VE GOT A PASSPORT FOR ME IN YOUR PURSE, I'M NOT GOING ANYWHERE.
I TOLD YOU, ZAN. I KNOW PEOPLE. WE CAN GET YOU A NEW ONE.
WE CAN'T, SOPH. I WISH I COULD EXPLAIN WHY.
BUT I CAN'T LEAVE. I HAVE TO STAY.
ZAN...
I'LL TEXT YOU IN A COUPLE DAYS. WE'LL DO THIS AGAIN WHEN I'M A LITTLE MORE HEALED UP.
BYE, SOPH.

ALMOST TWO MONTHS SINCE I GOT BACK AND I BURNED A FEW WEEKS IN THE HOSPITAL, GETTING MY FROSTBITE TAKEN CARE OF.
DRAGGING MYSELF OFF THE BRINK OF DEATH, THE WAY I DRAGGED MYSELF DOWN OFF THAT MOUNTAIN.
FOR THIS. TO BE HOME.

SURROUNDED BY REMINDERS OF WHO I USED TO BE.
INDIA
EVERYTHING I LOST.

ALL THE THINGS I CAN'T GET BACK.
HOME SWEET HOME.

THOUGH YOU REALLY CAN'T GO BACK AGAIN.
EVERYTHING'S CHANGED. EVERYTHING IS OMINOUS.
HALF-CONVINCED I'M BEING WATCHED. WAITING FOR THE MAJOR, THAT VOICE ON THE PHONE, THE FACE ON THE YOUTUBE CLIPS, TO STEP OUT IN FRONT OF ME.

MY JOB USED TO BE BEING WATCHED.
ONCE UPON A TIME I LOVED IT.

THEN I TRIED TO FADE OUT OF VIEW.
AND HERE I AM AGAIN, IN THE CROSSHAIRS INSTEAD OF A VIEWFINDER.
I'M NOT EMILY. I'M ZAN. ALWAYS WILL BE.

BUT I'M NOT ALONE.
I HAVE PEOPLE WHO CARE ABOUT ME.

OR CLOSE ENOUGH.
HELLO, DARLING, AND HOW WAS YOUR DAY?
LET ME IN, DANIEL.

WANT A DRINK?
SEVERAL. LET'S GET SHITFACED, HONEY.

ALL THESE PEOPLE, AND I CAN'T TELL A SINGLE ONE THE DAMN TRUTH. I CAN'T GET ANYONE ELSE HURT.

TO US.
UH-HUH.
EXCEPT MYSELF.

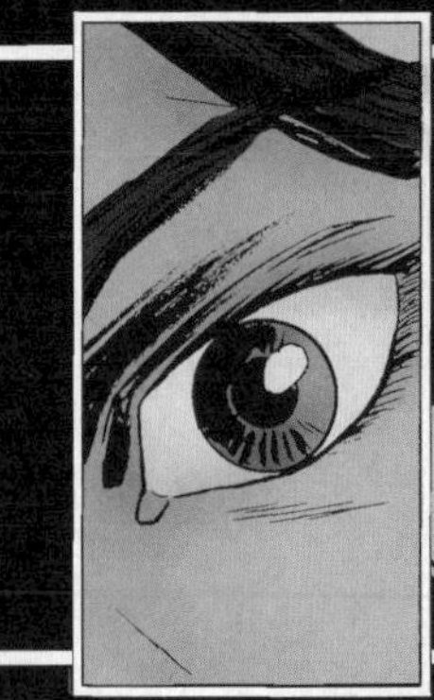

GODDAMMIT.
I HAVE THE DREAM EVERY OTHER NIGHT.
SOMETIMES EVERY NIGHT.

IT'S ALMOST A RELIEF TO WAKE UP TO MY LIFE.
EVERY TIME, EVERY NIGHT, I HAVE TO MAKE SURE THEY'RE STILL THERE.

THEY ALWAYS ARE. SOME NIGHTS I HOPE THEY WON'T BE.
THAT THIS WAS JUST ANOTHER NIGHTMARE.

BUT NO. I'M NOT THAT LUCKY.

MAYBE SOMEDAY I CAN DO SOMETHING WITH THEM. IF I LIE LOW LONG ENOUGH, IF I LAST LONG ENOUGH.
THEY'RE ANOTHER SET OF MEDALS. TINY BURDENS OF A PAST LIFE I'D RATHER NOT RELIVE.
I REFUSE TO GIVE THEM UP.

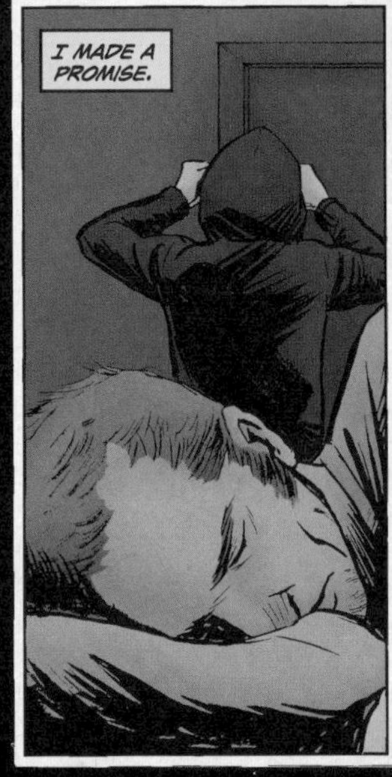
I MADE A PROMISE.

ONCE UPON A TIME, I FUCKED IT ALL UP.
CLIMB EVEREST
BUT I SURVIVED. AGAIN AND AGAIN.
I HAVE THAT ONE MOMENT.
MY HAND ON THE SUMMIT.
THE ROOF OF THE WORLD.

THEY CAN'T TAKE THAT AWAY.
THEY CAN'T KILL ME FOR IT.

IT'S MY LIGHT AGAINST THE DARK.

THE ROPE THAT KEEPS ME FROM FALLING.
I HOLD ON TIGHT.
LIKE I WAS TAUGHT.
THE END

HIGH CRIMES
BONUS FEATURES
Commentary by Christopher Sebela

This page: An alternate cover sketch for issue #1. *Next three pages:* "Strange Truths," a short story that ran in the Comic Book Legal Defense Fund's *Defend Comics*, a comic produced for Free Comic Book Day 2014.

"STRANGE TRUTHS"
- A HIGH CRIMES STORY -

Denny Ahern's second mistake was coming to Maryland.
His third was opening the door.
His first was ever getting as far as he did on this story. Taking a folder of disparate notes and photos on a dozen different subjects, turning them into a map of who really runs things in this country. How they do it. And why.
The why is always the most dangerous part.
Most people would burn their notes, get a job pumping gas. Most people, it would make them careful, hesitant, suspicious.
517
It just made Denny bolder. Desperate.
Like he knew, by turning that knob, what would happen.
He'd become immortal.
Not for anything he'd done in life, not for breaking this story wide open.
But for everything he could have done. Could have been right about.

SO WHY'D YOU DO IT, DENNY? WHY COME HERE?
JUS' DO IT ALREADY, G-MAN.
NOT UNTIL YOU ANSWER ME. WHY?
BECAUSE I KNEW YOU WERE COMING.
OR SOMEONE LIKE YOU.
ONCE I GOT TOO FAR, I KNEW YOU'D SHOW UP.
I BEEN PLANNING FOR IT. LOOKIN' FORWARD TO IT.
THERE'S CHEAPER WAYS TO KILL YOURSELF, DENNY.
NO, NOT LIKE THIS. MY PEOPLE'LL KNOW I DIDN'T DO THIS.
I BEEN DROPPING HINTS FOR MONTHS NOW.
EVENTUALLY SOMEONE'LL COME LOOKING. FOR THE STORY. MY NOTES.
PUT IT ALL TOGETHER. GET THIS STORY OUT THERE.
LET MY KID KNOW HIS DAD WASN'T NUTS LIKE THEY SAY.
HELL, I WAS STUCK ANYHOW.
THIS... THIS'LL MAKE 'EM PAY ATTENTION.
MAYBE SO, DENNY. MAYBE SO.
GO TO SLEEP.

A USER'S GUIDE TO *HIGH CRIMES*

DECLASSIFIED

If you want to get technical, the genesis of *High Crimes* stretches all the way back to 1852. Back then, a computer (an actual job title in the 1800s) named Radhanath Sikhdar smashed all the Great Trigonometrical Survey of India's measurements of the mountain designated Peak XV together and figured out that, at 29,000 feet above sea level, this peak was the tallest thing in the entire world. By the time the computers we're more familiar with showed up, they verified he was only off by 29 feet.

Once the explorers had conquered both poles, when there seemed to be nowhere man hadn't stood, they headed upward, to what was now known as Mount Everest.

It still took 101 years and two dozen lives lost before Edmund Hillary, a beekeeper from New Zealand, and Tenzing Norgay, his Sherpa partner, reached the roof of the world and, most importantly—just ask George Mallory and Andrew Irvine—made it back alive to tell the tale.

After that, the floodgates burst wide. It became about first and fastest, until Everest slowly transformed from a symbol of the impossible to a trophy. One few have collected, but growing crowds show up every year to pay tens of thousands of dollars to make their play for it, regardless of whether they belong there or if Everest wants them. Meanwhile, professional climbers thumb their noses at the mythical beast, referring to the popular southeast ridge approach as the "yak route," scoffing at its lack of technical challenges. Everest isn't hard to climb, they insist; it's merely hard to survive.

Still, there remains an Everest mania that infects its acolytes and draws them back, one failed summit after another, climbing beyond their limits, reaching the top only to have no way back down, ignoring the signposts of the frozen, half-buried bodies they pass all the way up. Every season, the number of climbers grows, and the number of bodies increases. Which leads to the other kind of mania, the armchair mania. This is mine. For years now—funneled through books, movies, and documentaries—I've gotten all the terror of Everest without having to leave my house.

That fixation, on their parts and mine, led to what's become *High Crimes*. While I would never want to climb Everest, I do want to understand those people who do. What makes someone stare up at the cruising height of a jumbo jet and think, "I want to go there"? Who would willingly enter an environment so hostile to life that the last few benchmarks exist in an area officially named "the death zone"? Who would pay the price of a new car to be given the very tools to survive and then turn their backs on help when they need it most? Is it all worth it to sit on a crowded cornice of snow-covered rock for twenty minutes as your brain and body slowly die?

High Crimes is, in its rough and bloody way, about this mania, about obsession and addiction, about that mutant breed of people comfortable wading into certain death—some for a paycheck, some for glory, some for mysterious urges not even they can explain. It's also about guns and violence, drugs and delusion, fame and infamy, illness and injury, and the human urge to go where everything around you is shouting, "Turn back."

In the end, the mania we studied and told stories about became our own. *High Crimes* is a book that Ibrahim and I have worked on for years. It was with us for marathon all-nighters in offices, studios, and coffee shops. We studied climbing videos and maps of Kathmandu to the point of memorization. We can tell you about each camp on the southeast route, down to the toilets and the tents and the fixed rope lines and the best time to pass through the Khumbu Icefall. Without even realizing it, we became obsessed, and neither of us will ever see a crampon or an ice axe the same way again.

Obsession can't be explained to an outsider. It becomes a secret language you only speak with others like you. It's found in calculating the trigonometry of heights or plotting the best route to the summit or fixing up a shot of morphine or uncovering the best way to tell a story. In the end, George Mallory answered as well as anyone could when it comes to the question of why: Because it's there.

Editor's note: This is an updated version of an essay that ran in High Crimes *#1.*

Cover process for issues #7 and #8 by Ibrahim Moustafa.

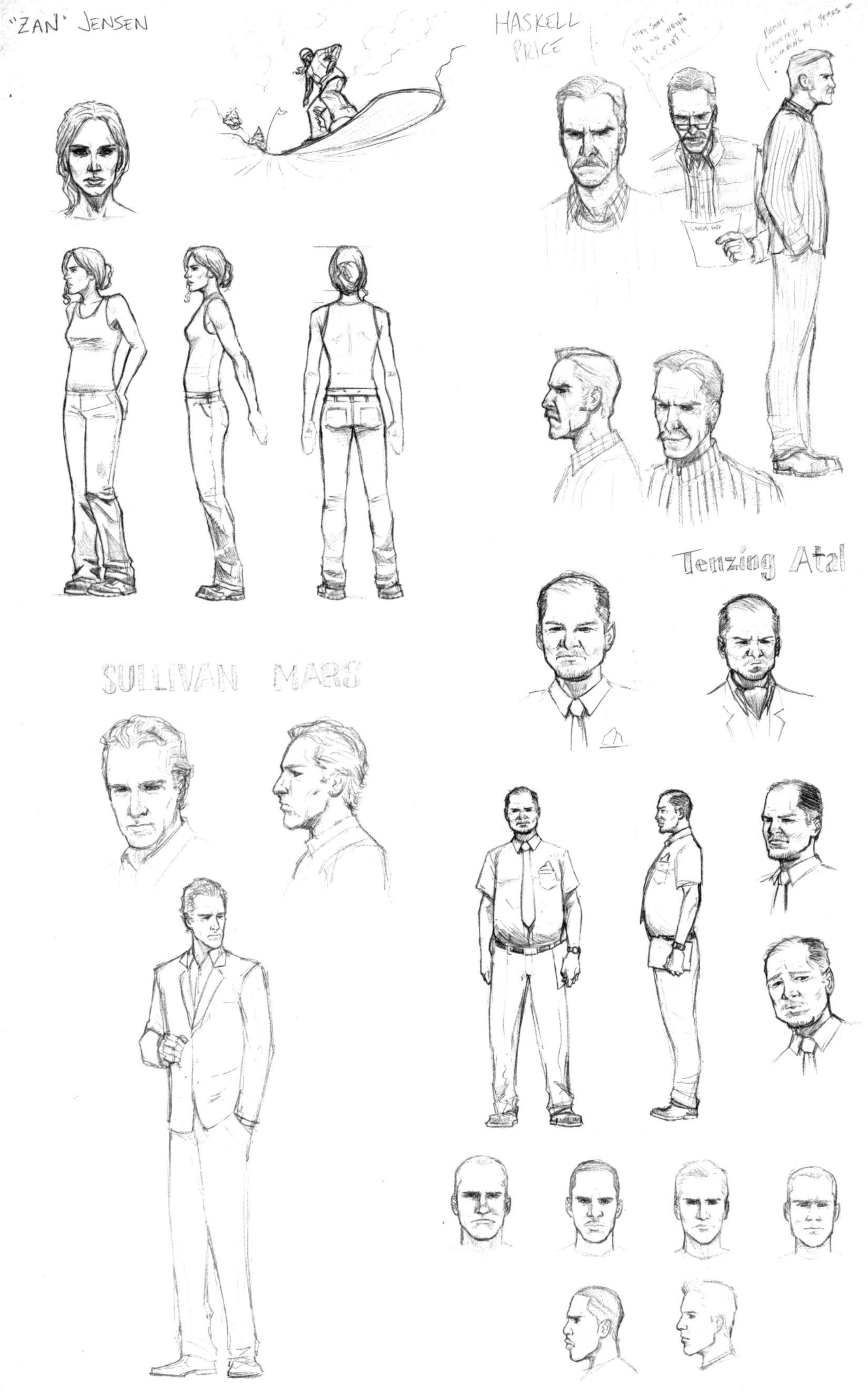

"ZAN" JENSEN

HASKELL PRICE

THEY SENT ME THE WRONG RECEIPT!

POSTURE AFFECTED BY YEARS OF CLIMBING

Tenzing Atal

SULLIVAN MARS

Initial character sketches by Ibrahim Moustafa.

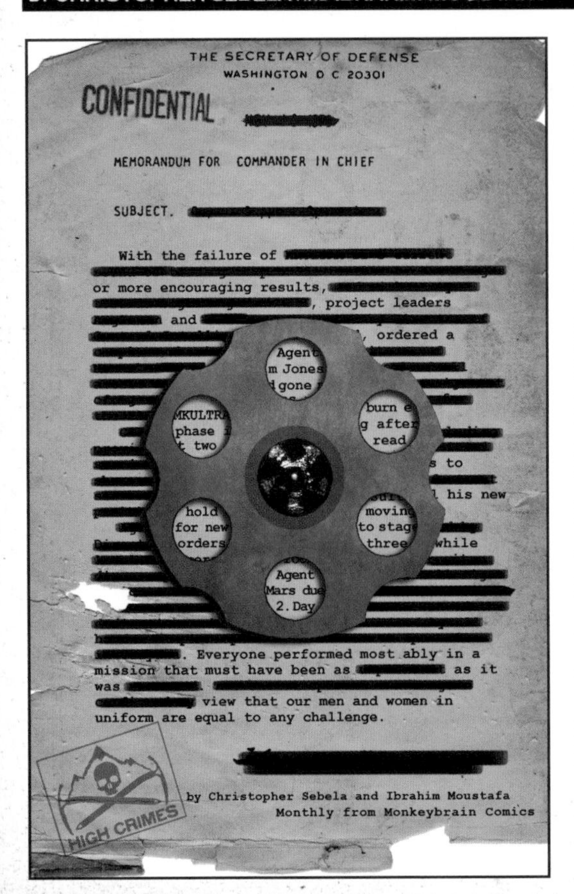

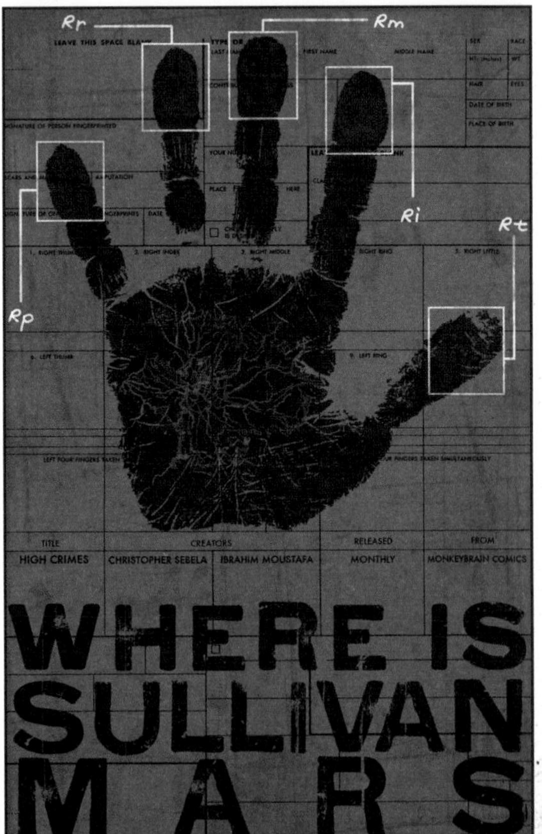
Rr
Rm
Ri
Rt
Rp
LEAVE THIS SPACE BLANK
TITLE
HIGH CRIMES
CREATORS
CHRISTOPHER SEBELA
IBRAHIM MOUSTAFA
RELEASED
MONTHLY
FROM
MONKEYBRAIN COMICS
WHERE IS SULLIVAN MARS

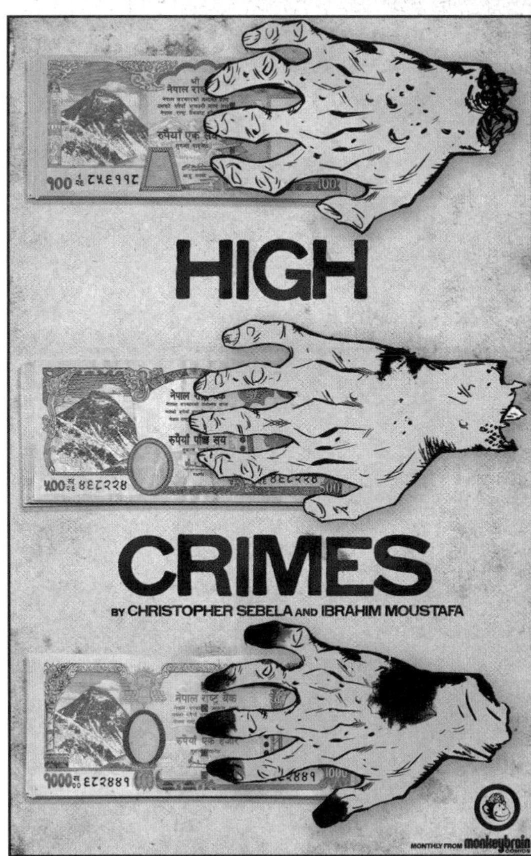

Eight days before *High Crimes* #1 was released, I got the genius idea to do a week of promotional pieces to tease it online. To make things harder on myself, I decided to do it as a numerical countdown, the first one having seven elements, the last one having just one. Seven was the Seven Summits—the tallest peak on each continent and the name climbers use for the achievement of conquering them all. Then came six chambers, five fingers, four characters, three severed hands, and our two partners. One (see following page) was always Everest herself, the biggest character in our book. These promos did the job, giving people an idea of what the book was about and the mood of what we were setting out to do without us having to spill all our secrets at once.

The final of the seven countdown promos.

Promo for *High Crimes* #3 featuring a hand drawing that was generously donated by artist Brian Churilla—which I used until the wheels came off.

Once everyone knew what the book was about, that was permission to have fun with the promos. Mostly I wanted to see if I could actually pull it off with any accuracy, so I did *High Crimes* as movie poster, as pulp novel, as comic book advertisement. I even made a Choose Your Own Adventure cover, but we didn't want to get sued.

Iconography was always really important to *High Crimes*. Ibrahim's covers were all very iconic and singular, and I tried to operate under his design philosophy when I was doing promos. So, to promote issue #5, I made prayer flags, which can be found all over Everest, especially flapping into threads at the summit. Then I put all our other major icons—the film, the gun, the knife, and the hand—inside them.

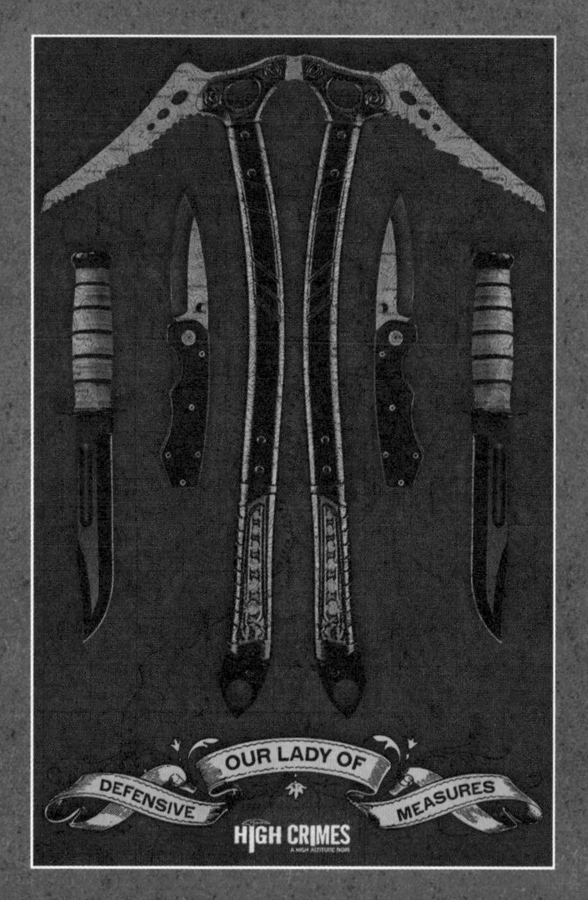
OUR LADY OF
DEFENSIVE
MEASURES
HIGH CRIMES
A HIGH ALTITUDE NOIR

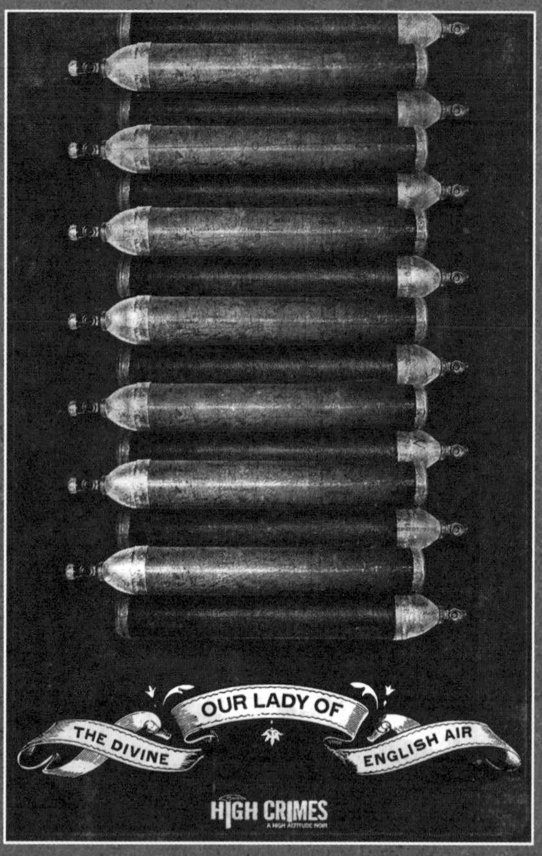
OUR LADY OF
THE DIVINE
ENGLISH AIR
HIGH CRIMES
A HIGH ALTITUDE NOIR

OUR LADY OF
CLOSE
CALLS
HIGH CRIMES

OUR LADY OF
IMPOSSIBLE
DREAMS
HIGH CRIMES
A HIGH ALTITUDE NOIR

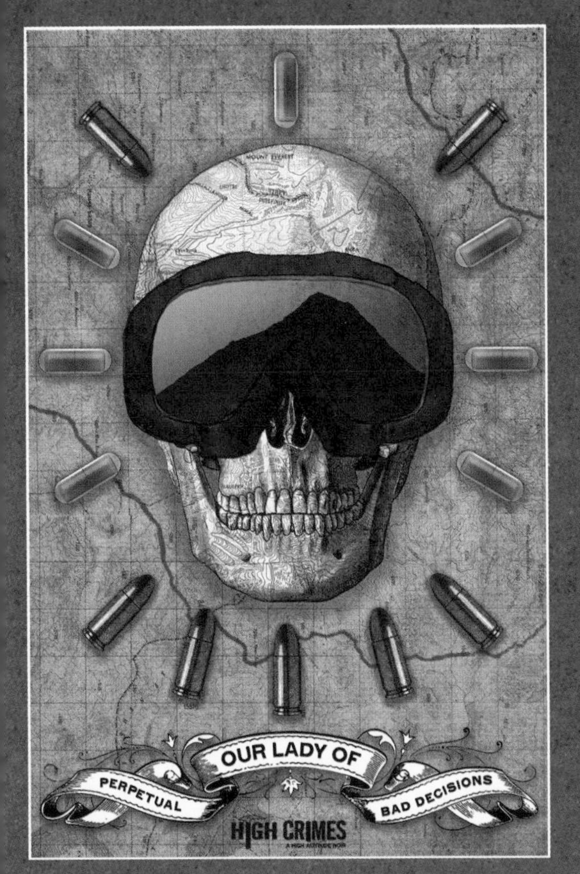

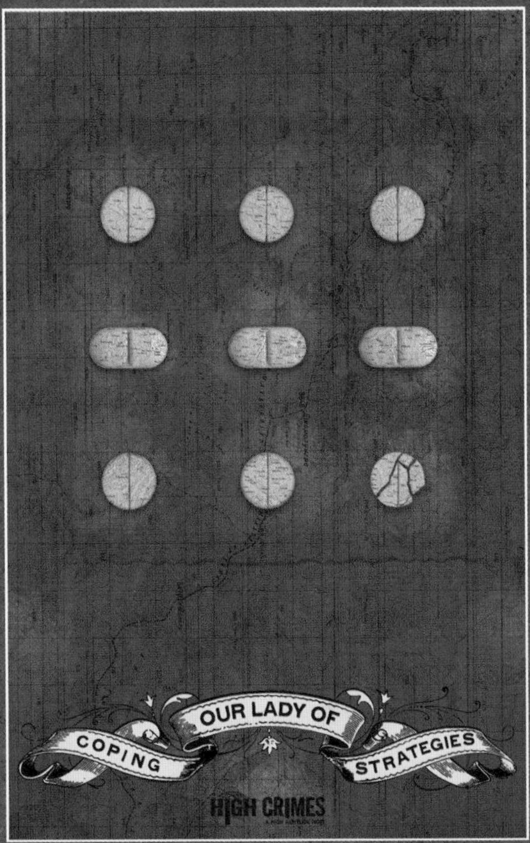

Patron saints of *High Crimes*. I had no solid idea in mind when I made the first one, except that I had to make one. It wasn't until I finished the second one that I realized these were all like holy relics of our book, and everything kind of fell into place from there. These were the hardest of the bunch to make, but they're the ones I like the most. Everest's recipe of suffering equals success is proven true yet again.

R AND ESPIONAGE

from Dark Horse Books

BLACKSAD

JUAN DÍAZ CANALES AND JUANJO GUARNIDO

The *Blacksad* books first took Europe by storm in 2000 and sold over 200,000 copies in France alone. Now Dark Horse presents the beautifully painted stories of private investigator John Blacksad, up to his feline ears in mystery, digging into the backstories behind murders, child abductions, and nuclear secrets.

ISBN 978-1-59582-393-9
$29.99

MIND MGMT VOLUME 1

MATT KINDT

A young journalist stumbles onto a big story—the top-secret Mind Management program. Her ensuing journey involves weaponized psychics, hypnotic advertising, talking dolphins, and seemingly immortal pursuers. But in a world where people can rewrite reality itself, can she trust anything she sees?

ISBN 978-1-59582-797-5
$19.99

THE BLACK BEETLE VOLUME 1: NO WAY OUT

FRANCESCO FRANCAVILLA

Follow Francesco Francavilla's critically acclaimed pulp hero the Black Beetle—Colt City's sleuthing sentinel—as he searches island prisons, dank sewers, and swanky nightclubs for the mysterious man known as Labyrinto.

ISBN 978-1-61655-202-2
$19.99

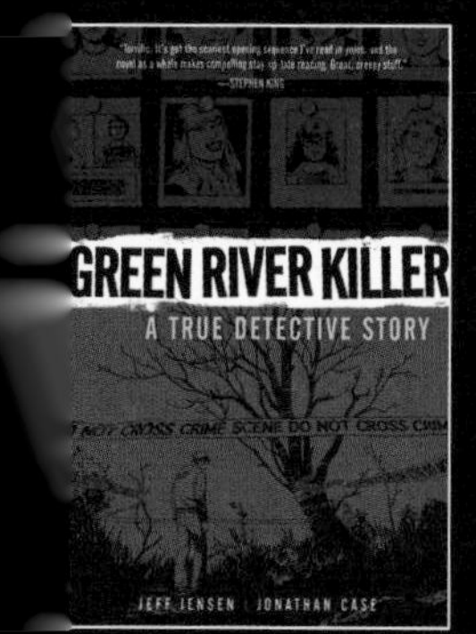

GREEN RIVER KILLER: A TRUE DETECTIVE STORY

JEFF JENSEN AND JONATHAN CASE

The story of one of America's most notorious killers is revealed in this true-crime comic unlike any other! Written by case detective Tom Jensen's own son, acclaimed entertainment writer Jeff Jensen, this is the ultimate insider's account of America's most prolific serial killer.

ISBN 978-1-59582-560-5
$24.99

LE AT YOUR LOCAL COMICS SHOP OR BOOKSTORE • TO FIND A COMICS SHOP IN YOUR AREA, CALL 1-888-266-4226

Rocky